THE SCARECROW AUTHOR BIBLIOGRAPHIES

R.C. HUTCHINSON

The Man and his Books

Scarecrow Author Bibliographies, No. 70

by
Robert Green

With a Foreword by Sir Rupert Hart-Davis

The Scarecrow Press, Inc.
Metuchen, N.J., & London 1985

Library of Congress Cataloging in Publication Data

Green, Robert, 1940–
 R.C. Hutchinson, the man and his books.

 (Scarecrow author bibliographies ; no. 70)
 Includes index.
 1. Hutchinson, R. C. (Ray Coryton), 1907–1975--
Bibliography. I. Title. II. Series.
 Z8429.48.G74 1985 [PR6015.U76] 016.823'912 85-2024
 ISBN 0-8108-1801-9

To Margaret Owen Hutchinson
with admiration and affection

CONTENTS

FOREWORD

One morning in September 1933 Hugh Walpole telephoned in great excitement: he had discovered a new novelist of genius. This happened so often that it was difficult for his friends to keep pace with his enthusiasms, but I must read this book, he said: it was called The Unforgotten Prisoner by R.C. Hutchinson, a name unknown to both of us. I did so, and was bowled over, just as Hugh had been. This long and appalling story of poverty and dereliction in the defeated Germany of 1919 must, I imagined, have been written by a man who had served in the British Army of Occupation and seen the horrors he so vividly described. Later I discovered that he had been eleven years old when the war ended.

Ray Coryton Hutchinson was born at Finchley on January 23, 1907, and educated at Monkton Combe School and Oriel College, Oxford. His first job was in the advertising department of Messrs. J. and J. Colman at Norwich, but he had always wanted to be a novelist, and he wrote assiduously every evening and weekend. In 1929 he married Margaret Owen Jones and in 1930 his first novel, Thou Hast A Devil, was published. In the same year his daughter Ann was born, to be followed by Jeremy (1932), Elspeth (1934) and Piers (1937). In 1935 he gave up his job and became a professional writer. Both his first novel and his second, The Answering Glory (1932), were what in his later military service he would have described as "sighting shots," but in The Unforgotten Prisoner he found his own very individual voice.

One Light Burning (1935) told of an explorer in the frozen wastes of Siberia, Shining Scabbard (1936) of a doomed French family in the provinces in 1914, and Testament (1938) of the Russian Revolution. This epic novel was chosen by the Book Society, and awarded the Sunday Times Gold Medal for Fiction. Hutchinson's stature as a novelist was now beyond question, but he had time to complete only one more novel--The Fire and the Wood (1940), an agonizing tale of a young German doctor and his tuberculous patient in the throes of the Nazi tyranny--before five years of service in the army halted his writing life. Three of his first four postwar novels--Interim (1945), Elephant and Castle (1949), and The Stepmother (1955)--were set in England, and though they have their fervent supporters, they seem to me to give him too little scope and to lack the force and impetus of his greater works, as though for

the full deployment of his vivid imagination he required a huge pano-
rama of catastrophe in a far country of which he had little or no
first-hand knowledge. This he achieved again in Recollection of a
Journey (1952), an almost unbearable account of the forced expatri-
ation of tens of thousands of Poles to Siberia, mostly on foot (he
excelled in descriptions of arduous journeys in hellish conditions),
and in March the Ninth (1957), a savage tale of postwar vengeance
in Yugoslavia.

With A Child Possessed (1964) he reached what seems to me
the apogee of his creative genius. This tale of the love of a Mar-
seilles lorry driver for his idiot child is a work of great beauty and
compassion, with the underlying assumption, which permeates all
Hutchinson's works, that Christian love is the only hope for the
world. This book gained him the W.H. Smith Literary Award and
was everywhere received with respect, if not always with complete
approval.

His last (unfinished) novel, Rising (1976), set in South America in 1903, maintained his highest standard. All the best novelists
create their own world, into which the reader enters with absorption.
Hutchinson did this, but in each of his major works the world is a
different one, wholly apposite and convincing. He was a creative
writer if ever there was one, and though an uneven writer with occasional failures, I claim that of his sixteen novels at least seven are
major works, fit to stand beside the finest novels of this century in
any language.

Altogether five of his novels were chosen by book clubs in
Britain and in America, and individual books received magnificent
reviews, many of them by fellow-novelists. Compton Mackenzie
wrote: "R.C. Hutchinson is the best male novelist his generation
has produced. We know what we mean by poetry and by genius,
and I find authentic evidence of both in One Light Burning." Storm
Jameson called Hutchinson "the finest living novelist," and he was
praised by, among others, Walpole, Priestley and Edwin Muir. Yet
in the endless stream of books, articles and discussions about the
modern novel and contemporary literature I have never once seen
his name mentioned. All his life, regardless of fashion, neglect or
misunderstanding, he pursued his solitary way, taking no part in
what is called literary life, attending no parties--a dedicated artist
if ever there was one. R.C. Hutchinson is not the first great
writer who has had to wait for posthumous recognition and continued
readership, and both, I am convinced, will come to him sooner or
later. In the last few years his works have indeed found a new generation of readers: a selection of his short stories was published in
1984 and almost all the novels are again available in paperback.
Genius is impossible to define, and the word has become tarnished
by exposure, but I believe R.C. Hutchinson had it.

Dr. Robert Green's book is the one we have been waiting for, since it provides exactly what was needed to educate the public, the critics and the professors. Hitherto it has been difficult to assemble information about R.C. Hutchinson and his books. Now all the basic facts are here clearly set out in detail. I am sure this is a sign that at last the tide of neglect is turning, and the fervent admiration of a few will soon be shared by many.

I cordially recommend Dr. Green's book. After you have read it, read all Hutchinson's work you can get hold of. I envy you your thrill of recognition.

Marske-in-Swaledale   Rupert Hart-Davis

PREFACE

This reader's first acquaintance with the work of R.C. Hutchinson dates from 1977 when, quite by chance, I came across a copy of Rising, the novel on which he was at work when he died in the summer of 1975. Though uneven in achievement, Rising is undoubtedly a work of 'epic' proportion and of high ambition: it was set in 1903-1904, the same years in which Joseph Conrad was writing Nostromo, and it shares with the latter boldness of vision as well as a South American setting. Rising, then, whetted my appetite and I wanted to read the rest of Hutchinson's fiction and to find out something about the novelist who had suddenly and powerfully surprised me.

My surprise, however, continued when I discovered that the other sixteen novels were difficult to obtain (none at that time was available in paperback); and, furthermore, that very little had been written about Hutchinson's achievement in the standard histories of twentieth-century fiction. Rising had, I knew, been short-listed for the Booker Prize as recently as 1976, and its author had carried off other awards in 1966 (for A Child Possessed) and in 1938 (for Testament), yet virtually nothing had been written about his work, and his name was scarcely mentioned in the reference books on the modern English novel.

Now, some seven years later, the position has greatly improved: most of the novels are available in paperback editions and a selection of Hutchinson's short stories has also been published. His work, too, has been featured on the BBC in 1976, 1981 and 1982, and written about very perceptively in London Magazine. Moreover, a splendid edition of Hutchinson's correspondence with the poet Martyn Skinner was prepared by Sir Rupert Hart-Davis in 1979. These are all important stages in the growth of Hutchinson's reputation, and this book is intended to confirm the increasing interest in his work.

The availability of a reasonably complete checklist, both of what Hutchinson himself wrote and of the reviews that he received from October 1930 to the present, is an essential basis for critical evaluation, and it is for the use of critics, rather than book collectors, that the present work is mainly designed. One such critic, John Bayley, reviewing March The Ninth in 1957, remarked that Hutchinson had always been "a baffling but oddly impressive writer." Other critics too, before and since, have reacted in similarly hesitant

ways when confronted with Hutchinson's fiction. One source of the
lack of critical attention paid his work, quite apart from the writer's
own unwillingness to publicize himself, has undoubtedly been this difficulty in 'classifying' his work, for, if he is not, or not primarily,
a 'literary' novelist like Murdoch or McEwan, nor is he a straight-
forwardly 'popular' writer like MacLean or Monsarrat. We cannot begin to answer such questions properly, cannot start to 'place' Hutchinson within the context of twentieth-century English fiction, until we have looked at the whole of his output, from the short stories
written at Oxford in the late-'twenties down to the posthumously
published Rising. The present book, for the first time, enables
that kind of reappraisal to begin, for it lists and locates everything
that Hutchinson published between January 1928, when the first
story appeared in The Empire Review, and 1976. (The entry on
Hutchinson in Contemporary Novelists listed only four of the twenty-
eight published short stories, and incorrectly dated editions of four
of the seventeen novels.)

   Most of the present book, then, consists of material essential
to any critical evaluation of R.C. Hutchinson. It is divided into
three sections--Published and Unpublished Works, and Secondary
Material--and within the first two primary sections, Hutchinson's
work is listed by genre. The entries on Hutchinson's published
novels list all the major editions, translations, dramatizations, as
well as the sources for manuscripts and typescripts. Similar details
are provided for his other creative work: his short stories, a play
and a military history commissioned at the end of the war. Much of
Hutchinson's nonfictional prose--the articles, reviews and talks--is
inevitably of rather limited interest, but I have nevertheless chosen
to list everything he published, indicating with an asterisk material
particularly relevant to an understanding of his fiction. The unpublished material in Section Two is, again, divided by genre. The
third and final section of the checklist is devoted to secondary material, a list of the general studies of Hutchinson's work (and studies
of individual works with a broad applicability) being followed by reviews of his various works, a memoir by a contemporary, and a short
section in which are included the miscellaneous press reports that appeared about the novelist's life and work. In this part, in the list-
ing of reviews, I have been forced to be highly selective and it is
necessary to explain here the principles by which, for example, only
twenty-one of the ninety-nine reviews available of Testament have
been cited and annotated. The overriding criterion for inclusion was
simply the quality of the review itself, the reviewer's insight into the
text and the permanent value of the commentary. In addition, though,
several other criteria were employed: the usefulness of publishing
hostile as well as laudatory reviews, thus aiming at some kind of
balance; secondly, the value in recording how the major critical out-
lets (such as The Times Literary Supplement in England and the
New York Times Book Review in America) and the period's major
critical voices (among others: Walter Allen, Richard Church, John
Cournos, Alfred Kazin, Day Lewis, Edwin Muir, Sean O'Faolain, J.B.

Priestley, V.S. Pritchett, Stephen Spender, Frank Swinnerton and Sir Hugh Walpole) reacted to Hutchinson's fiction. And quite apart from the intrinsic interest of this section to the student or biographer of R.C. Hutchinson, it also serves to document modulations in critical taste and in the style of fiction reviews over the last fifty years. Finally, wherever possible, samples of American notices have been included alongside the major British reviews. All the reviews included here by these various criteria have been annotated, and in some cases lengthy quotations have been provided as well. And, in the Appendix at the end of this volume, I have reprinted three of Hutchinson's critical essays on the grounds that the little criticism he did write is very difficult to obtain outside specialized academic libraries. All this bibliographical material is preceded at the beginning of the volume by a few "Biographical Notes" and a critical introduction charting the various stages in the novelist's career.

My acknowledgments span three continents. In America, I have been greatly assisted by Ellen S. Dunlap, former Research Librarian of the Humanities Research Center at Austin, Texas, who was kind enough to mail me information about the Center's holdings of Hutchinson material. In Africa, where the typescript was prepared, I thank the Research and Publications Committee of the University of Malawi for its financial assistance, and the university authorities and its English Department, under Professor Adrian Roscoe, for permitting me the luxury of a term's leave of absence. Finally, in England, I am delighted to acknowledge the helpfulness of Peter Day, Michael Joseph's editor who was working on the text of Rising and first introduced me to the novelist's widow; the persistence of Mrs. A.V. Mason of Virgo Books, South Wraxall, for tracking down several of the more elusive of Hutchinson's works; the kindness of Sir Rupert Hart-Davis, long an admirer of Hutchinson's fiction, who is in the midst of a hectic 'retirement' provided the Foreword to this volume, offered invaluable suggestions as to its presentation, and corrected several errors of fact. Above all, though, I acknowledge the unstinting generosity of the book's dedicatee, Margaret Owen Hutchinson, who allowed me access to all her late husband's papers, which she either mailed to me in Malawi or permitted me to work on in her London apartment. Without Mrs. Hutchinson's hospitality, enthusiasm and encouragement, this book would have been impossible.

Robert Green
Kwaluseni,
Swaziland.
June 8, 1984

Abbreviations

The following abbreviations have been employed:

HRC   Humanities Research Center, Austin, Texas
MOHC Collection of Margaret Owen Hutchinson

BIOGRAPHICAL NOTES

1907	January 23	Ray Coryton Hutchinson born in Finchley, North London.
1920		Educated at Monkton Combe School, near Bath, where he writes a 20,000 word novel, "The Hand of the Purple Idol."
1927		M.A., Oriel College, Oxford. Joins the Advertising Department of Colman's, Norwich.
1928	January	His first publication, a short story, "Every Twenty Years," in Empire Review.
	September	Begins writing Thou Hast A Devil.
1929		Marries Margaret Owen Jones, daughter of Captain Owen Jones, C.B.E.
	January	Completes Thou Hast A Devil.
	February	Second short story published in English Review--"A Rendezvous for Mr. Hopkins."
1930		Writes "The Caravan of Culture," his only unpublished adult novel.
	October 3	Thou Hast A Devil, his first novel, published in London. At work on The Answering Glory.
1931	December	Begins writing The Unforgotten Prisoner.
1932	March 3	The Answering Glory, the second novel, published in London.
	June 6	The Answering Glory is published in New York and is a Book-of-the-Month Club recommendation.
1933	March	Completes third novel, The Unforgotten Prisoner.
	December 4	The Unforgotten Prisoner published in London, where 15,000 copies are sold in the first month.
1934	February 6	The Unforgotten Prisoner published in New York.
1935	February	Fourth novel, One Light Burning, is published in New York and in London, where it is a best seller. Leaves Colman's and starts writing full time.
1936	September 10	Fifth novel, Shining Scabbard, published in London.

	December 28	Shining Scabbard published in New York. Again a book club recommendation. 78,000 copies sold in two weeks.
1938	August 11	Last Train South opens in a West End theatre.
	September 3	Last Train South closes after poor notices.
	September 5	Testament, the sixth novel, published in London; a Book Society choice.
	October 24	Testament published in New York.
	November 14	Awarded Sunday Times "Gold Medal for Fiction."
1939		At work on The Fire and The Wood.
1940	February	The Fire and The Wood completed.
	March	Commissioned in the Army.
	June 6	The Fire and The Wood published in London, where it is a Book Society choice.
	June 20	Signatory to PEN Declaration for international support against Nazi Germany.
	July	Posted as Captain, 8th Battalion, East Kent Regiment ('The Buffs').
	August 30	The Fire and The Wood published in New York; a Literary Guild selection there.
		"Designs" Elephant and Castle.
1943		Staff College, Camberley.
		Begins Interim.
1944		Serves in War Office, London.
	December 4	Writes the speech delivered by King George VI at the Stand-Down Parade of the Home Guard.
1945	March	Interim, his eighth novel, published in London.
	April	Begins to write Paiforce in Baghdad.
	May	Interim published in New York.
	July	Completes Paiforce.
	October	Demobilized with rank of Major.
		Attends some sessions of the War Crimes Trial at Nuremberg.
1946	January	Begins writing Elephant and Castle.
1948		Elephant and Castle completed.
	September	Visits New York to publicize Elephant and Castle.
		Begins writing Recollection of a Journey.
1949	January 27	Elephant and Castle, the ninth novel, published in New York. First printing of 25,000 copies with a further 170,000 for book club.
	January 28	Paiforce, a military history, published in London.
	April 26	Elephant and Castle published in London, where it is a best-seller.
1951		Recollection of a Journey completed.
1952	January 14	Begins The Stepmother.
	April 27	Recollection of a Journey, his tenth novel, published in New York as Journey With Strangers.
	October 23	Recollection published in London.

1954	September 9	Completes The Stepmother.
1955	April 20	Begins March The Ninth.
	August 19	The Stepmother, Hutchinson's eleventh novel, published in New York. Book club recommendation.
	September 8	The Stepmother published in London.
1957	April	March The Ninth is completed.
	October 28	March The Ninth published in New York.
	November 4	March The Ninth published in London, where it is a selection of the Book Society.
1958	January 13	Begins Image of My Father.
	November	Adaptation of The Stepmother plays in London's West End.
1959	May	Visits Belfast.
1960	November	Image of My Father is finished.
1961	September	Image of My Father, the thirteenth novel, is published in London and is a Book Society recommendation.
1962	January	Image published in New York as The Inheritor; Book club recommendation.
	June 7	Elected Fellow of the Royal Society of Literature.
1964	September	A Child Possessed published in London. Begins work on Johanna.
1965	January 27	A Child Possessed published in New York; his fourteenth novel and a book-club recommendation.
	June 26	Delivers speech at the annual meeting of the English Association.
1966	November 9	Receives W.H. Smith Literary Award for A Child Possessed.
1969	April 28	Johanna at Daybreak published in London, the fifteenth novel.
	September 24	Johanna published in New York, a book-club recommendation.
1971	March 21	Begins work on Rising, his last novel, during a boat trip to South America.
	September	Origins of Cathleen published in London only, after rejection by American publishers.
1975	July 3	R.C. Hutchinson dies, leaving the final chapter of Rising incomplete.
1976	September 6	Rising published in London only.
	November 4	Rising is short-listed for the Booker Prize.

R.C. HUTCHINSON: A CRITICAL INTRODUCTION

The recent paperback reprint of Hutchinson's long novel about the Russian Revolution, Testament, marks a further stage in the uneven history of that work. First published in September 1938, it won the Sunday Times Gold Medal for Fiction in November, and a fifth edition appeared as quickly as January 1939. There was then a seven-year gap before the sixth edition in May 1946, soon after the wartime restrictions on paper had been lifted. Seventeen more years elapsed before its reissue by Duckworth in 1963, and Testament did not appear in paperback until November 1981. It is strange that a novel which was a critical and commercial success in 1938 should have been neglected for so long, but this indeed was the pattern of R.C. Hutchinson's career as a whole. Spurts of recognition would be followed by years of anonymity: Johanna at Daybreak was a book-club recommendation in America in 1969, yet his next two novels, Origins of Cathleen (1971) and Rising (1976), both failed to find American publishers. A writer's career often falls into a recognizable shape: Hutchinson's was mysteriously inchoate.

Ray Coryton Hutchinson was born in Finchley in 1907. He was educated at a public school near Bath, and it was here that he wrote an unpublished novel, a juvenile thriller gaudily entitled "The Hand of the Purple Idol." For some months after his sixteenth birthday he also kept a diary in which he inscribed his adolescent pessimism, differences with his deeply evangelical father and the ephemera of schoolboy quarrels. (February 28. "Have put a poem in 'The Monktonian' which will rather settle scores with young Jeremy, on the Corps business.") A couple of entries that summer also noted his enjoyment of Balzac's Poor Relations, which "seems damned good; but inhuman in some respects." (June 10, 1923) He enjoyed Balzac's "excellent technique, clear (but I cannot think brilliant) style, and good humour. Characters very well done, and motive well worked out." (June 17, 1923) This entry ends: "I really enjoyed every page of it, so much so that I finished it in the week; which is a testimony of slackness. Impetigo not much better." Hutchinson's early acquaintance with, and admiration for La comédie humaine is of particular interest, for his work was later to be compared with Balzac's.

Three entries from the diary also establish the schoolboy's growing interest in socialism, as well as his skin trouble:

> The spirit of French Rev. was socialism, and social-
> ism is or should be the great ideal. (February 8, 1923)

1

> I am getting more and more convinced about social-
> ism. You know we <u>must</u> give everyone a chance.
> They are not like ourselves, but they are made in
> our likeness. (February 27, 1923)
>
> In town today [during the Easter vacation].
> <u>Gorgeous</u> Blackfriars. Yes, the class system must
> go; it is mucking everything. Each hols tell me
> the same thing. (April 5, 1923)

Monkton Combe School was probably not a socialist hotbed in
1923, and indeed the last entry suggests that his holidays in London perhaps made a deeper impression than any of his reading or
classes at school. It was clearly a socialism tinged with Christianity
and with the conventional public-schoolboy's <u>noblesse oblige</u>, the
adolescent idealism recorded in a mixture of schoolboy slang and
Marxian fragments. Still, Hutchinson's sensitivity to the inequities
of London was to endure and to form the basis of <u>Elephant and
Castle</u> (1949).

Several other entries that year record his ambition to write a
novel. On the day after his sixteenth birthday he felt that he had
the "materials for a best-seller" but doubted that his style would "go
down" (January 24, 1923). This may be a reference to the unpublished "Purple Idol" and indeed part of the reason for keeping a
diary was to record ideas that he would later be able to draw on for
his fiction. One entry in particular takes us beyond the juvenile
story and allows us to glimpse the adult novelist in embryo, already,
at the age of sixteen, demonstrating some of the humanity and power of observation characteristic of his mature fiction. Early in
March he visited Bath Abbey with an aunt and wrote about this
trip:

> What interests me most are the little stones, tucked
> away behind the big ones; very few people seem to
> notice them. 'Here lies Mary Smith. Born 1716.
> Died 1773.' What was Mary Smith like, I wonder.
> Possibly the Abbey charters would have something
> about her. (March 8, 1923)

The "little stones" of this entry are recognizable prototypes
of Hutchinson's later heroes, common men and women pushed
hither and thither across the surface of twentieth-century Europe,
mere pawns in the hands of the Nazi and Soviet authorities. Hutchinson's adult fiction was to be engaged in reconstructing what
such lives were "like," employing all the resources of his own imagination, plus, as the last sentence of the Bath entry hints, the
combing of available documentary evidence, what Hutchinson was to
call the novelist's "donkey work." These few lines already sketch
the various stages behind the writing of his adult fiction: the ini-
tial moment of curiosity, followed by the effort to imagine and re-

construct, supplemented by recourse to printed sources. The veri-similitude for which Hutchinson was to be so often praised was achieved by a combination of the novelist's intuition anchored by detailed and laborious research. The notebooks he kept for his last novel, Rising, serve to confirm the interdependence of these twin activities.

After leaving school Hutchinson went up to Oxford, where he rowed in the Oriel boat, flew in the University Air Squadron, and studied. (Among his contemporaries at Oriel were the historian A.J.P. Taylor, Harold Hobson, the theatre critic, and the novelist and critic, J.I.M. Stewart.) He also continued to write fiction, for his first published short story, "Every Twenty Years," was written while he was an undergraduate though it did not appear until January 1928, after Hutchinson had gone down. From Oxford he joined Colman's of Norwich where he worked in the Advertising Department, popularizing mustard, from 1927 to 1935. His first novel, Thou Hast A Devil (1930), a futuristic fantasy, was little noticed and is now virtually unobtainable, though the Times Literary Supplement remarked on its author's "vivid imagination" and a provincial reviewer was convinced by the accuracy of Hutchinson's vision of the future:

> ... certainties, such as television and private aero-planes, a possibility, such as a regular airship service to the Far East, and wilder flights of fancy [sic], such as self-rule for negroes, all fit neatly into place without impeding the course of the story.

Hutchinson may have been a powerful prophet, but this was the last occasion he looked to the future: the rest of his novels were to be reconstructions of the recent past. Thou Hast A Devil was set in an undated future, yet its linguistic and social conventions were very much those of the English bourgeoisie of the late 'twenties. In 1953, looking back on his first novel, Hutchinson dismissed it as "a wad of balderdash."

The Answering Glory, published in London and New York in 1932, was better received. The story of the courage of a woman missionary posted to an island off the African coast attracted favorable attention in New York, but has never been reprinted. Hutchinson's career as a novelist was really launched the following year with the publication of The Unforgotten Prisoner (1933), of which 15,000 copies were sold in London within a month of its appearance. Highly praised by Hugh Walpole and by Compton Mackenzie ("the best English novel ... published this year, and one of the half-dozen best English novels written since the War"), The Unforgotten Prisoner was the first of Hutchinson's many attempts to transmit to an English readership the horrors of continental Europe in the twentieth century. Much of the novel was set in Germany in the early 'twenties, with war, famine and mass unemployment being seen through the eyes of a young German orphan.

Hutchinson published one more novel before leaving commerce to devote himself full time to literature. One Light Burning (1935) was another portrait of individual heroism, battling against a harsh environment, its hero an academic philosopher searching for a friend lost in the Arctic. Bonamy Dobrée praised its "terrific narrative drive and profound understanding," and Rayner Heppenstall its "largeness of conception and fullness ... of reality." "Definitely," his review ended, "Mr. Hutchinson is competing with the giants of literature." L.P. Hartley, too, found in One Light Burning "literary and imaginative power of a high order." Hutchinson's first four novels had, then, been increasingly well received, and he was still only twenty-eight when, having written the early chapters of a fifth, Shining Scabbard, and emboldened by his wife, he abandoned the security of advertising.

So far the pattern is familiar enough: five short stories and three essays preceding the first of the two 'apprentice' novels, which are then confirmed by two novels of greater confidence and maturity. Yet an interesting feature of Hutchinson's early years is the novel he did not publish: no 'young man's novel,' no fiction derivative of his own experiences at university and in commerce. (An 'epistolary' novel of this period, which was set in England, "The Caravan of Culture," remains the one novel of Hutchinson's maturity that failed to find a publisher. Ironically, it was also the only novel he designed as a 'pot-boiler.') Instead, the major characters of these early works--a woman missionary, a German orphan--are plainly invented, and their settings alien, even exotic. Also noteworthy is the promptness with which the young novelist located what would be a permanent interest in the theme of endurance under suffering: Alan Wild of One Light Burning and the young Klaus are the ancestors of many of Hutchinson's later heroes, men and women who face and surmount the worst physical and mental obstacles.

Still only twenty-nine, but now married, settled in the Cotswolds and writing full-time, Hutchinson published his fifth novel, Shining Scabbard, in the following year, 1936. The decision to retire early from commerce had already been justified by the sales of his novels and it may be worth dwelling briefly on the economics of authorship in the 'thirties. Hutchinson's first literary earnings had in fact been recorded as far back as 1917, when, aged ten, he had received from Lady Haig two guineas for a prize-winning essay on "War Models." Eleven years later, the first short story brought him Ł9 and his income from stories and essays was only a little more the following year. Thou Hast A Devil, the first novel, netted Ł26 in 1930, supplemented by Ł30 for stories and non-fiction. In 1931 he was at work on Answering Glory and thus earned little, but in 1932 his income from writing rose to Ł240, the English and American advances on his second novel. This fell back to less than Ł100 in 1933, yet next year, his last at Colman's, he made nearly Ł900, a considerable sum, most of that being the English royalties on Unforgotten Prisoner. In 1935, the first year of full-time writing, Hutchinson

made over ₤700 and between 1935 and 1939 his literary income averaged nearly ₤1,100 per year. At a time when young men in the pro-
fessions married and began a family on ₤300 a year, Hutchinson's
decision to write as a career had already been justified. These details have been taken from the account books in which, for nearly
forty years, Hutchinson would meticulously record every penny and
cent of his authorship; he was always proud that from his earnings
he had been able to put four children through university.

Shining Scabbard, a resounding success in England and in
America, is a long, leisurely portrayal of the musty obsessions of a
bourgeois family in provincial France just before the First World
War, remarkable for the skill with which Hutchinson drew foreign
characters and an unfamiliar environment. Again war--the Franco-
Prussian conflict for Colonel Séverin, with the 1914 war darkening
the lives of his bullied children and grandchildren--is the touchstone
by which man is measured. Shining Scabbard evidently caught the
public's sense of foreboding in 1936, the year that saw the remili-
tarization of the Rhineland and the beginning of civil war in Spain,
for it was a best-seller in London as well as in New York, where
78,000 copies were sold within two weeks. It was acclaimed by
Pamela Hansford Johnson, J.B. Priestley and by Sir Hugh Walpole,
who, the following year, included Hutchinson among the three most
"promising" English novelists, the others being Graham Greene and
Christopher Isherwood. In another survey in 1937 Woolf, Huxley,
Maugham and Wells were adjudged the major English writers, but
Hutchinson was included alongside David Garnett, Wyndham Lewis
and E.M. Forster as those with "a hint of greatness." His sixth
novel, Testament, would be received as the work of a young novelist who had already built a considerable reputation.

The publication of Testament, however, was preceded by
Hutchinson's first, and last, stage play. Last Train South, set in
a railway station in Russia in 1919-1920, was clearly a by-product
of his current preoccupation with the 1917 Revolution. Starring
Flora Robson and produced by Basil Dean and J.B. Priestley, it ran
in the West End for three weeks. One of the few reviewers to welcome the play was Harold Hobson, who saw in Hutchinson a recruit
to the English theatre "whose intensity of feeling, clarity of perception, and dramatic skill are qualities of the highest potential value." Hutchinson's strength as a playwright was not to be tested
again, yet the existence of several play scripts among his unpublished work suggests that the failure of Last Train South had not
unduly deterred him.

Testament was published two days after the play closed and
its reception must have consoled Hutchinson for the disappointment
in the theatre. Several of the period's leading reviewers--Day Lewis,
Frank Swinnerton, Kate O'Brien, Edwin Muir and Douglas Goldring
in England; John Cournos and Alfred Kazin in the United States--
responded with great admiration, the novel's critical and commercial

success being reflected in the award of the "Sunday Times Medal for Fiction." Testament was quickly translated into Swedish, German and Norwegian, but its criticism of the Bolshevik regime ensured that it has never been available to Russian readers. Elsewhere its success was based on the novel's intense moral seriousness, on Hutchinson's superb narrative gifts and, again, on his ability to invest a foreign setting with the power of actuality. (One of his 'fan letters' was from an English nurse who had been working in Russia in 1917 and insisted that the novelist must also have been there.) Though he had no first-hand knowledge of the country, Testament felt so 'Russian' that one reviewer called Hutchinson "a literary chameleon of overwhelming talents." Alfred Kazin, similarly, wrote of the novelist's "amazing virtuoso's gift, his aptitude for running over European boundary lines, for seizing a stranger's speech, for binding himself to the world's occupation." Constance Garnett, whose own translations had made the Russian classics available to English readers, was another of Testament's admirers.

At the outbreak of war, then, Hutchinson's position at the forefront of English fiction was secure, with Testament amply confirming his earlier promise. This reputation was based on his willingness to undertake the ambitious task of rendering civil war and revolution in terms that were comprehensible to a readership without firsthand experience of dislocation and anarchy. As Frank Swinnerton put it, Hutchinson was remarkable for his courage in attempting a large canvas and a great theme. There is no doubt that the materials on which he chose to work significantly extended the range of English fiction in the 'thirties. The Fire and The Wood (1940), the last novel he completed before being claimed by the army, also engaged with a major theme, the rise of Nazism in the 'thirties and its repercussions on the lives of a Jewish doctor and his gentile, tubercular patient. Hutchinson had begun The Fire and The Wood in 1938, but the outbreak of war meant that he could no longer command the leisure that had enabled him to find unhurried conclusions for Testament and Shining Scabbard. Like them, The Fire is a novel of intense moral seriousness, but there is some evidence that its later pages were affected by the novelist's need to complete the work before he was commissioned.

Hutchinson served in the army from March 1940 until October 1945, at first in Buckinghamshire and Devon as a Captain in the Buffs, then at Staff College, Camberley, and in the War Office in London. As he remarked later, the army treated him "with exceptional charity," and "no one who, physically fit in 1939, found himself in the same physical condition at the end of 1945, has the smallest excuse for grumbling about his lot." Nevertheless, despite the characteristic lack of self-pity in Hutchinson's gratitude at surviving the war unscathed, these five years did steal from him the opportunity to produce much fiction: the momentum built up by Testament and Shining Scabbard was unavoidably lost. Lack of time was particularly crucial for a novelist who always maintained that the writing of fiction was "a slow form of art," in which novelists "by using a very great number of small, skilful strokes ... have gradually, slowly, brought the whole man to life." For five years in his mid-thirties Hutchinson was deprived of the time that had earlier enabled him to accumulate such "whole" characters as the Séverins or the Otraveskovs, and the one novel he did write during the war, Interim (1945), was uncharacteristically brief. It was aptly titled, for in several respects Interim is concerned with interruption, disjunction and intermission, both in the lives of the novel's characters and its author's unsettled existence, having been written late at night in 1943-1944, with the antiaircraft guns shaking Hutchinson's top-floor Kensington room. Interim appropriately marked the halfway point in Hutchinson's career: it was his eighth novel, and nine postwar novels were to follow it. Meditative, subjective, even perhaps partly autobiographical, Interim is unusual among Hutchinson's fiction for the absence of any extensive, ramifying plot, and for the small cast of characters it deploys.

When Interim was published in March 1945 Hutchinson was already at work on a very different project, a history of the Persia and Iraq theatre of operations that had been commissioned by the War Office. He spent several months in the Middle East on this book, marvelling at the immense logistical complexities of the whole Persian operation, which enabled five million tons of war matériel to cross a thousand miles of desert and mountain between the warm waters of the Persian Gulf and the Russian border far to the north. So many diverse units and skills were deployed in "Paiforce" that, as its historian noted, "the interlocking of all these activities has the beauty of an elaborate machine in motion." Between the lines of Paiforce (1949) one senses an affinity between the intellectual dexterity of the military commanders in Persia and the novelist commissioned to record their skills, ones similar to those utilized in the construction of a novel as complex as Testament.

Hutchinson developed a great respect for the officers and men of "Paiforce" and, in return, these months in Persia offered him the germ of one of his best postwar novels, Recollection of a Journey, which ends, like Paiforce, with the arrival in the Gulf of shiploads of Polish refugees. These civilians, appearing anonymously in the military history wearing "old overcoats and shapeless trousers, torn shawls and faded gabardines, boots falling to bits, nondescript wrappings of greasy flannel and tattered linen," were to be transformed by 1952 into the Kolbeck family of Recollection of a Journey. This was one of the rare occasions in Hutchinson's career when a novel incorporated, with few adjustments, some of his own experiences.

However, before Hutchinson could make any progress on Recollection, for which he had already discovered a conclusion, he had to return to Elephant and Castle, a voluminous novel of London working-class life he had started to "design" in 1940. An undated entry in his "Plots Book" reveals its embryo:

> Girl who 'reclaims' criminal and marries him. Criminal does not respond. Gradually revealed that criminal has the real virtues, honesty, etc, while girl is really moral poseuse.

This gradual revelation of the true characters of Gian, the "criminal," and of his middle-class wife, Armorel, sustained over nearly 700 pages of text, was what impressed Elizabeth Bowen when she read Elephant and Castle, so different from her own practice in The Death of the Heart. It had to be a long novel, she noted, because "its action covers nearly twenty years, its theme is formidable and its exploration of the soul requires space." Elephant and Castle also elicited an excellent review from Alex Comfort, and this piece, though written over thirty years ago, remains one of the most perceptive essays ever written on Hutchinson. Comfort's conclusion was that Elephant "has the scale of a major novel, its technique and its observation match that scale, and its total success is uniform enough to make it comparable with other major work." Elephant and Castle was also an outstanding commercial success in America and in Britain, where sales even rivalled those of the recent translation of Mann's Dr. Faustus.

The completion of Elephant in 1948 allowed Hutchinson to return to Recollection of a Journey, which he had started in Baghdad three years earlier. In this novel, his sixth with a setting of continental war and revolution, Hutchinson set himself the task of imagining the experiences of one of the many Polish families he had seen disembarking in the Gulf since September 1939, when war began and Recollection opened. The "Table of Events" he drew up for Recollection stretched back, though, as far as 1847, when Stanislas Kolbeck was born, so that he was here attempting to imagine the lives of an aristocratic Polish family over nearly a hundred years. Recollection's historical ambition is matched by the novel's technical boldness, for Hutchinson elected to tell this story through the eyes of the Polish heroine, a more difficult business than employing an omniscient, third-person narrative. In one of his notes he meditated on the style required, both by the nightmarish quality of the events recounted and by the femininity of Recollection's perceiving consciousness:

> The style must have the quality of limpidity. It must have a music. It must be flexible, so as to carry factual matter and descriptions of sordid realities as well as subtle descriptions of psychical states. But above all it must, in itself, represent the hallucinatory feeling of the story. It must also be feminine.

Hutchinson's achievement in Recollection of a Journey was that, as in The Unforgotten Prisoner and Testament, he communicated to English and American readers the full horror of war and revolution in continental Europe. Recollection was at the same time both "factual" and "hallucinatory," and, as Stephen Spender remarked, "a wonderful vindication of the power of the novel to hold up a mirror to the most confusing events of our time." Spender's use of Stendhal's metaphor here also serves to remind us of Hutchinson's kinship with the masters of nineteenth-century realism, though his narrative recounts horrors of a quite new dimension. These, the refugee's experience of uprooting and exile, of successive harassment by both Fascist and Communist invaders, are all of them being remembered in the comfort of Stefanie's postwar sanctuary, distanced in space and time from the nightmares of war. Hutchinson had already employed this device, the remembering narrator, in Testament, where Otraveskov is recalling the Russian Revolution from a Parisian flat in the mid-'twenties and he was to use it again most powerfully in Johanna at Daybreak (1969). Here, as in Recollection, the heroes are obliged to relive some of their wartime experiences before they can begin to live positively in peacetime. The value of reminiscence as therapy is central to Hutchinson's perception of the relationship between the past and the present. The past cannot be escaped: it can only be remembered and decoded as the basis for renewal.

Recollection of a Journey was completed in 1951 and so Hutchinson had used the six years since his demobilization to produce two very long novels, which made immense technical and emotional demands. His next novel, The Stepmother (1955), was written between January 1952 and September 1954, almost, it seems, as a form of diversion from the recent intense preoccupation with the totalitarianism and mass suffering of the 'forties. He has recorded how, after completing Recollection, he took up this theme again, but was unable to bring it to a conclusion:

> A year's work on a novel, exploring from a standpoint of Christian philosophy, the character of a woman responsible for gross atrocities in a concentration camp, went into the wastepaper basket and I turned to an entirely different theme and wrote The Stepmother. But the problem which the discarded novel tried to solve remained in my mind, as did my impressions of the ordinary and respectable appearance of most of the men and women accused at the International Military Tribunal at Nuremberg.

No trace remains of Hutchinson's work on this novel, but what Arendt called "the banality of evil" continued to preoccupy him in March The Ninth and Image of My Father until its fullest treatment in Johanna (1969). The latter was Hutchinson's final attempt to explore the theme of war guilt, yet even in Rising, the novel he was writing when he died, he is evidently still fascinated with the dynamics of guilt and reparation, though here these have been transferred to a South American setting at the beginning of the century.

The Stepmother was, then, something of an escape from a major emotional and intellectual fascination with the images of Auschwitz and Nuremberg. (At the invitation of Geoffrey Lawrence, later Lord Oakley, Hutchinson had attended some of the trials there in 1945.) In Testament and Recollection the novelist had been working with 'epic' materials, with revolution, war and homelessness, the characteristic modern traumas, and working, moreover, at epic length. By contrast, The Stepmother is spare, concentrated, the most "intimate, personal and private" of Hutchinson's novels, with most of its action internal and subjective. Nevertheless, there are points of contact with his earlier works, for Hutchinson is here still concerned with, in Norman Shrapnel's words, "the weight and the deviousness of biography, with the complicated burden that the past imposes on every human life." The Stepmother's 'history' has been 'domesticated,' a private family history, but it retains its power to shape the present.

Hutchinson spent the next six years, from 1955 to 1961, working on the wider implications of history, perhaps taking up and recasting some of the features of the novel he had discarded. The two novels of this period, March The Ninth (1957) and Image of My Father (1961), are both set soon after the war, and investigate the individual's attempt to understand the immediate past, of war and genocide, and relate it to the present. At a period when much English fiction and poetry was determinedly low-keyed, ironic and insular, Hutchinson retained an unfashionable interest in the larger issues of history and morality; recounting the tribulations of a provincial academic held no attractions for him. March The Ninth tells how a surgeon in Trieste in 1947, working peacefully for an international relief organization, becomes implicated with a wounded ex-Nazi and his wife who are on the run. The doctor has to decide how much he owes to the past, to the rationality and justice of his duty to reveal the fugitives' hiding place to the police; and how much to the present, to the claims of a wounded man and a woman with whom he is inconveniently in love. The novel was designed to illuminate just those moral problems, of guilt and loyalty, generated by war and unsolved by peace. The faces of Nuremberg's accused are visible between its lines. War and the deracination it produces is also the central experience of Image of My Father, where Hutchinson returns to one of the themes of The Unforgotten Prisoner, the contrast between the mores of the English bourgeoisie, ignorant of invasion and occupation, and those of Belgians who had suffered war more directly. "A novel about the natural history of a man called Selborne," Image of My Father narrates the efforts of Selborne's unacknowledged Belgian son, Vincent, to discover his father's identity. Involuntary service in a German labor unit had broken Vincent's marriage and driven him into callous egotism. His quest for his father is one part of his search for a way out of darkness and despair.

Despite its serious theme, the evidence from Hutchinson's Account Books suggests that the sales of Image were disappointing and, furthermore, that his last five novels, from Image to Rising, attracted many fewer readers than, say, Testament or Recollection. By the late-'thirties, as we saw, he had built up a considerable readership, and Elephant and Castle (1949) undoubtedly refurbished Hutchinson's reputation after the war. This novel and Recollection (1952) were indeed so successful that between 1949 and 1953 his income averaged well over Ł3,000 a year. The Stepmother and March The Ninth were not quite as lucrative but nevertheless from 1954 to 1961 Hutchinson's average income was around Ł2,600 a year. Image was published in 1961 (1962 in America) and Hutchinson's combined income for the next two years failed to reach four figures. (Thus for 1962 and 1963 he earned less than in 1934 and in 1935--much less in real terms--when he had just begun to write full time.) Another significant fact is that March The Ninth was the last of his novels to be a book-club selection, though three of the next five were recommendations. It seems certain, then, that his readership was beginning to desert him in the late-'fifties and early-'sixties and that nothing he wrote in the 'sixties was to reverse that trend. True, he won a major literary prize in 1966--and commented, significantly, that it "strengthens my morale at a time when that recruitment is much needed"--but there is no evidence that the sales of any of the last five novels approached those of Testament before the war, or of Recollection or Elephant and Castle in the early 'fifties.

It is difficult to understand why Hutchinson's reputation declined after March The Ninth. Certainly the last five works reveal no loss of literary ability, for, although Origins of Cathleen was an attempt to work a new genre, comedy, the preceding novel, Johanna, was as powerful as anything Hutchinson ever wrote; and Rising, the last work, made a magnificent conclusion to his long career. One possible clue to the novelist's decline can perhaps be discovered in the terms he himself used to describe the importance of fiction in the speech accepting the W.H. Smith Prize in November 1966. "The novel," he said on that occasion

> only comes to its full stature when it defies every
> determinist philosophy, when it accepts the mys-
> terious, the numinous, when it recognizes in every
> human being not only a marvellous machinery but
> also a unique and divine creation.

Hutchinson had, of course, held these views for many years, but his employment of fiction as a means of embodying his Christian principles may have been increasingly unwelcome to readers in the 'sixties and 'seventies. His persistence in treating the major issues of the century in novels that were serious, even moralistic, and always tinged with his belief in the possibility of salvation through endurance, may well have made him seem old-fashioned to a new generation. Perhaps Hutchinson felt something of this, for in a letter written in 1974 he described himself as a "passé author," though the novel he was then writing, Rising, shows no loss of power.

Hutchinson's fourteenth novel, A Child Possessed (1964), the winner of the W.H. Smith Prize and the immediate occasion for his comments on fiction's need to be hospitable to the numinous, certainly illustrated the limits of any narrow positivism. The rationalism of the neurological surgeons dictates that Eugénie, a mongol child, ought to undergo a brain operation to ameliorate her condition, and ought to remain institutionalized. At the beginning of the novel Hélène, her mother and a celebrated diseuse, shares this view, that "human lives need to be ordered by shrewd negotiation and sensible decisions," but Stepan, the child's father, vetoes the operation and removes his helpless, deformed daughter from the Swiss hospital. Before the end of the novel Eugénie has quite transformed her parents, whose experience of nursing her will, it is hinted, reunite the estranged couple. A Child Possessed aimed to demonstrate that the "goodness of God ... can find a passage through every human absurdity and every corruption," and it is the novel's achievement that this is managed with no trace of the sentimentality unavoidable in any crude paraphrase of the plot. The moral issue of the novel, an examination of the responsibility towards a mongol child of its parents and medical attendants, was given a sustained treatment in 1964, many years before this complex issue could be aired publicly in Britain.

A Child Possessed was completed in 1964 and Hutchinson then began work on Johanna at Daybreak. That it was not finished until 1968 is revealing of both the difficulties Johanna posed as well as the sixty-year-old novelist's inability to write at great speed. Testament, a much longer novel, had been written in two years, yet Johanna undoubtedly posed substantial artistic problems and, as James Fenton remarked in his review, the novel is

> most remarkable on sheer technical grounds, for its
> handling of a given true [sic] story so that there
> is no otiose material, and for the gradual revela-
> tion of the truth through the uncertain and ambigu-
> ous point of view of the narrator, which develops
> through stages of fear, isolation, resignation and
> despair towards something verging on hope.

The story of Johanna is actually fictitious, but this review is nevertheless correct in the emphasis placed on the technical skills Hutchinson demonstrated here, his ability to distinguish between several different kinds of memory. Johanna Schechter, his narrator, is recalling her memories of the recent past, a few years after the war, when she had lived in a Dutch transit camp, and with her children in Germany. Behind this period, though, lies her memory of life just before the war, part of which (marriage to a prosperous Jewish editor, children, her own career) is intact, and part (betrayal of her husband to the Nazis, and the abandonment of her children) suppressed. Johanna, then, like Ford's The Good Soldier, juggles real memories, repressed ones, and even illusory memories,

hindsight's superimposition of present knowledge onto past ig-
norance, our rewriting of the past. The reader is drawn into this
kaleidoscope to reconstruct Johanna's real history as, step by step,
her past emerges from the darkness of normal forgetfulness and
from behind the screen she had erected to hide her own treachery.
In the powerful third part of Johanna this screen is wrenched aside
and the narrator is forced to relive the ultimate human degradation:
the betrayal of one's husband to perish in Dachau and the desertion of
one's children. However, once these events have been reexperienced,
through the simulated reenactment of two earlier interrogations, Johanna can begin to acknowledge her responsibilities and grope towards rehabilitation. Albrecht, the relative who had forced her to
release what had long been refused, admission of her own guilt, as-
serts at one point:

> No one's life can be divided into past and present
> with a thick line ruled between the two ... we're
> made out of our own history ... our past experi-
> ence and the way we've dealt with it.

Johanna at Daybreak is a novel of reconstruction, of the individual's rebuilding of a shattered psyche, and of the physical re-
creation, the 'economic miracle,' of postwar Germany. It is a sustained fictional achievement of very high order, a towering commentary on modern European history that will one day be properly
assessed as a classic of our time.

The Times Literary Supplement review of Johanna saw that
Hutchinson's novels

> stretch away behind him through three decades,
> spaced out like massive and stately mansions along
> some private avenue where nobody walks but he.
> They are spacious, constructed by a dedicated
> craftsman quick to reject anything shoddy or faked,
> and are all immediately recognizable as the work of
> the same hand.

This was a generous tribute to Hutchinson's lonely integrity,
marking him off from fiction's 'jerry-builders,' but the craftsman so
praised was now in poor health--angina had been diagnosed--so that
'bricklaying' was increasingly onerous, and only two more residences
were to be added to the estate, Origins of Cathleen (1971) and Rising. In a letter to Martyn Skinner, Hutchinson wrote revealingly of
his attitude towards these two novels:

> To clear the cobwebs I'm doing a mainly comic nov-
> el [Origins] at present. Quite hard and tricky
> work, and I have no idea whether anyone will find
> it at all entertaining. But I find a strange enjoyment
> in doing it. A more serious and much more ambi-

> tious book [Rising] is gathering, so to say, be-
> hind it. That one is one I very much want to
> write--it has a terrific ending (if I can find the
> right words). But it's a bit unlikely that, even if
> I survive, I shall have the mental guts to see the
> thing through. Already I feel old age clamping
> down on me--I find myself uttering old-gentlemanly
> remarks of deep disapproval about every new thing
> which happens.

Origins was subtitled A Diversion and it is plain from this letter that Hutchinson indeed regarded it as a way of recharging his
batteries, gathering strength for his assault on the last unclimbed
peak. In fact Origins had first been mooted as early as Spring
1962, when he wrote in his notebook:

> ?Next novel. English family. Fairly comic but pro-
> found. Autobiographical--perhaps written as if it
> were my own autobiography. Amused but affection-
> ate.

Sustaining a comic novel was a fresh challenge, though most
of his novels, even the darkest, are punctuated by comic, even
farcical episodes. (The horrors of Johanna are occasionally lightened
by inefficient taxis and misplaced suitcases.) Nevertheless the few
reviews Origins attracted in London were generally appreciative of
Hutchinson's attempt at a "comic but profound" novel. (Six American publishers rejected it on the grounds that it was too slow and
intricate for their market.)

By this time Hutchinson was already hard at work on Rising,
the novel planned as his final statement. Early in 1971 he and his
wife visited South America, the only occasion when Hutchinson visited a place specifically to gather material, and an indication of the
seriousness with which he approached the novel. By November of
that year he was describing how Rising was taking shape:

> At the moment I am all tied up with a very large
> list of characters. (Yes, they are supposed to live
> somewhere between Iquitos and Antofagasta; but
> somehow the scenery keeps wandering about rather.
> When mountains get in the way I move them a hun-
> dred kilometres east or west, hoping the reader
> will be too sleepy to notice), with appallingly com-
> plex thoughts and relations, lives which mean a
> great deal to me and with which, I fear, no pub-
> lisher, let alone the 'general reader,' will have any
> patience.

Hutchinson evidently found Rising extremely difficult to write--
it would have been a prodigious task for a young novelist in good

health--and in the summer of 1973, some twenty-seven months after
he had begun it, he commented:

> I'm making heavy weather of it. I've bitten off
> more than I can chew. The supposed reader has
> long been fast asleep and snoring (as I often snore
> myself, after trying to wrestle with one of Proust's
> longer and more involved disquisitionary para-
> graphs). I do three or four sentences a day: at
> sixty-six, and feeling ninety, with various trivial
> ailments that other men sensibly ignore, I tire
> easily.... At least a third of the book--at a rough
> guess--is still to be done. I gravely doubt if any-
> one will publish it. In some inexplainable, perhaps
> masochistic, way I still rather enjoy this ridiculous
> activity.

Progress on Rising evidently continued to be slow, for the
novelist's death, two years later, found the last chapter incomplete.
The notes he was making on the novel, though, allowed his widow
to suggest in a "postscript" that Hutchinson had intended Rising,
as the title implies, to end on a note of muted triumph, similar in
mood to the conclusions of Johanna and A Child Possessed. Hutchinson's comment in 1969, two years before he had even started the book,
that he envisaged for it "a terrific ending," must also encourage us
in our confidence that the appended Postscript accurately mirrors
his intentions.

The notebook for Rising indicates the immense dedication with
which the ailing novelist approached his last work. It is divided into twelve sections and amongst the "Principles" Hutchinson wrote
that he wanted to impart a "somewhat Proustian" quality to the family relationships. (He was, as we saw, reading Remembrance of
Things Past during Rising's composition.) The De Juanos family
should evince "a certain lack of intimacy, perhaps, but a tired, de-
fensive sense of holding together in a common cause." Reading
Proust and travelling 17,000 miles were supplemented by study of
the histories by Fawcett and Prescott, Blakemore's recent geography
of Latin America (1971), Che Guevara and Mao Tse-Tung's Gucril-
la Warfare, and the former's Bolivian diary. A prodigious quantity
of research, preparation and thought preceded Rising.

However, Hutchinson's inability to complete the novel ensures
that the most valuable entries in the notebook are those in which he
recorded his intentions in writing, the overall pattern of the narrative. His design for Rising was that it should demonstrate three
"forces" in operation:

(i)   x [Sabino]--representing power/status/wealth
      (roughly)

(ii) the form of revolutionary protest, headed by

>   an intelligent, resolute, ruthless man [Atun
>   Papac]
> (iii)   the ultimately winning force of love represented
>   by y [Qura Papac]

Within this algebraic pattern Hutchinson was aware of the danger of delineating the power of love too heavily. Instead, he noted, it should be

> hinted at--planted delicately--all the way through
> the book. It is the one which x cannot cope with
> because of his spiritual poverty, of which he is always
> vaguely aware--and for which he compensates
> by violence.

In another notebook, in which he jotted down details of places visited in South America, he wrote:

> One wants to show finally Reo Papac's influence
> overcoming the revolutionaries as well as Sabino; to
> suggest that one solution is always waiting, to be
> applied to every problem of conduct, political, social, etc.

And yet although Hutchinson's design for Rising had to ensure the final triumph of a peaceful, divine love, he was also conscious of the need to present the alternative, socialism, with fairness:

> It is of the first importance to delineate carefully
> the idea of violent revolution against that of revolution-by-love.
> The violent revolutionary's ideas--
> impatience, despair, practicality, etc: etc:--must be
> carefully and sympathetically studied.

The fullness and specificity of the notebook entries go far to compensate for the absence of Rising's last few pages. They also enable us to understand why Hutchinson attached such importance to his South American novel. The inspirational, healing power of love had been vital in his fiction from the very beginning--Guy Columbus' love for the faithhealer Khamhaïv in Thou Hast A Devil; Otraveskov's for the saintly Scheffler in Testament; Eugénie's power to transform her parents in A Child Possessed; Johanna's devotion to Tilka--so that in a sense Rising just confirms and recapitulates the intention presiding over Hutchinson's fiction from the start. At the same time, though, it is quite different from any of his earlier works, distinguished by what can only be described as a quality of exultation in its prose. His determination to complete Rising, planned as his final testament as early as 1969, lends to the prose an incandescence and a frenzied clarity so that the novel assumes, as The Times Literary Supplement noted, "a mythic proportion." Rising may not be Hutchinson's most perfect novel, but it is certainly his grandest and most joyful. The novelist, one friend felt, "had reached a sort of ecstasy in finding the story panning out so exactly in accordance with his own high ideals--and ... for an artist," he concluded, "that is not a bad moment to die."

On July 3, 1975, Hutchinson interrupted his work on the conclusion of Rising to welcome a couple of old friends to his Redhill home; he died later that day. The Times obituary was respectful ("he had a high reputation among a discerning public"), but its marked lack of enthusiasm probably only mirrored the critical consensus of the day: that Hutchinson was a worthy, albeit dated, novelist. A few days later Sir Rupert Hart-Davis, a longtime admirer, was moved to supplement the paper's appreciation and to establish Hutchinson's importance in twentieth-century letters. His advocacy was both fervent and disinterested, though interestingly Sir Rupert's conclusion returns full circle to some of the very earliest comments on Hutchinson's work in the 'thirties, when he implies that his fiction will be more highly regarded some time after his death, perhaps when it has been placed against the development of the English novel in the middle of this century. It is not too soon for the achievement of R.C. Hutchinson to be properly recognized.

SECTION ONE: PUBLISHED WORKS

A. Novels

    1. Thou Hast A Devil
    2. The Answering Glory
    3. The Unforgotten Prisoner
    4. One Light Burning
    5. Shining Scabbard
    6. Testament
    7. The Fire and the Wood
    8. Interim
    9. Elelphant and Castle
    10. Journey with Strangers (Recollection of a Journey)
    11. The Stepmother
    12. March the Ninth
    13. Image of My Father (The Inheritor)
    14. A Child Possessed
    15. Johanna at Daybreak
    16. Origins of Cathleen
    17. Rising

A.1. THOU HAST A DEVIL: A FABLE
      First English Edition
           Ernest Benn, London: October 3, 1930; 320 pages, 7/6d.
           (Author's name given as Ray Coryton Hutchinson.)
      Second English Edition
           Cassell, London: June 1935; 3/6d.
      Manuscript
           Manuscript, dated "September 1928--January 1929," in
           HRC.
      Binding Variants
           The first issue of the first edition was bound in good black
           cloth lettered in gold on the spine. Probably very few
           copies were sold, most of the others disappearing into cir-
           culating and other libraries. Part of the rest of the edi-
           tion was bound up in cheap red cloth, lettered in black on
           the spine. The black copies are now even harder to locate
           than the red ones.

A.2. THE ANSWERING GLORY
      English Edition
           Cassell, London: March 3, 1932; 320 pages, 7/6d.

American Edition
  Farrar and Rinehart, New York: June 6, 1932; 303 pages,
  $2.00.
  (Book-of-the-Month Club Recommendation, June 1932.)
Italian Translation
  As Vocazione, by Alessandra Scalero; Arnoldo Mondadori
  Editore, Milan: 1946; 304 pages, Lire 250.
Manuscript
  Manuscript in HRC.

A.3. THE UNFORGOTTEN PRISONER
  First English Edition
    Cassell, London: December 4, 1933; 529 pages, 8/=.
    (Book Society Choice, December 1933.)
  American Edition
    Farrar and Rinehart, New York: February 6, 1934; 564
    pages, $2.75.
  Canadian Edition
    O.U.P., Toronto: February 6, 1934; 564 pages, $2.75.
  Second English Edition
    Penguin Books, Harmondsworth: April 1983; 564 pages,
    £3.95.
  Dutch Translation
    As Morgenstond, by Willy Corsari; Zuid-Hollandsche Uit-
    geversmij: 1934.
  Hungarian Translation
    As Orok fogoly, by Maria Ruzitska; Singer és Wolfner,
    Budapest: 1941.
  German Translation
    As Der Unvergessene; Scherz-Verlag, Bern: 1944.
  Manuscript
    Manuscript, originally titled "Towards Morning," in HRC.

A.4. ONE LIGHT BURNING: A ROMANTIC STORY
  English Edition
    Cassell, London: February 1935; 376 pages, 7/6d.
  American Edition
    Farrar and Rinehart, New York: February 28, 1935; 340
    pages, $2.50.
    (Book-of-the-Month Club Recommendation, February 1935.)
  Canadian Edition
    O.U.P., Toronto: February 28, 1935; 340 pages, $2.50.
  Manuscript
    Manuscript, originally titled "Alan Wild," in HRC.

A.5. SHINING SCABBARD
  First English Edition
    Cassell, London: September 10, 1936; 506 pages, 8/6d.
  American Edition
    Farrar and Rinehart, New York: December 28, 1936; 483
    pages, $2.75.
    (Book-of-the-Month Club Selection, January 1937.)

Canadian Edition
O.U.P., Toronto: December 28, 1936; 483 pages, $2.50.
Second English Edition
Duckworth, London: 1968; 382 pages, 35/=.
(With an Introduction by Richard Church.)
Third English Edition
Zenith Books, London: October 1983; 399 pages, Ł3.50.
Swedish Translation
As Med Blank Varja, by Hakan Bergstedt; Bonniers, Stockholm: 1945.
Manuscript
Manuscript in HRC.

A.6. TESTAMENT
First English Edition
Cassell, London: September 5, 1938; 732 pages, 9/=.
(Book Society Choice, September 1938. Sunday Times
Gold Medal for Fiction, 1938.)
American Edition
Farrar and Rinehart, New York: October 24, 1938; 696
pages, $3.00.
Canadian Edition
O.U.P., Toronto: October 24, 1938; 696 pages, $2.75.
Second English Edition
Cassell, London: 1946; 15/=.
Third English Edition
Duckworth, London: August 15, 1963; 732 pages, 35/=.
Fourth English Edition
Duckworth, London: 1980; 732 pages, Ł12.50.
Fifth English Edition
Penguin Books, Harmondsworth: November 19, 1981; 732
pages, Ł3.95.
Swedish Translation
As Testamente, by Thorsten Jonsson; Bonniers, Stockholm:
1939; Kr. 15.00.
German Translation
As Ein Testament, by Maria Giustiniani; Bermann-Fischer
Verlag, Stockholm: 1939; Swiss Fr. 9.90.
Norwegian Translation
As Testamente, by Margrethe Kjaer; Gyldendal Norsk Forlag, Oslo: 1939.
French Translation
As Testament, by Erna Delile. Two volumes: Vol. I, Le
Soldat; Vol. II, L'Homme; J.H. Jeheber, Geneva: November 1944, June 1945.
Spanish Translation
As Testamento, by Luis de Caralt; Barcelona: 1945.
Manuscript
Manuscript in HRC.

A.7. THE FIRE AND THE WOOD: A LOVE STORY
First English Edition

Cassell, London: June 6, 1940; 418 pages, 9/6d.
(Book Society Choice, June 1940.)
American Edition
Farrar and Rinehart, New York: August 30, 1940; 440
pages, $2.50.
(Literary Guild Selection, September 1940.)
Canadian Edition
O.U.P., Toronto: August 30, 1940; 440 pages, $3.00.
Second English Edition
Readers' Union, London: June 1941; 2/6d.
Third English Edition
Duckworth, London: July 1970; 418 pages, 45/=.
Abridgement
In Redbook Magazine, LXXV, v (September 1940).
Manuscript
Manuscript, dated "February 1940," in HRC.

A.8.   INTERIM
English Edition
Cassell, London: March 1945; 143 pages, 7/6d.
American Edition
Farrar and Rinehart, New York: May 1945; 186 pages,
$2.00.
Canadian Edition
O.U.P., Toronto: May 1945; 186 pages, $2.50.
French Translation
As Intermède, by Jeanne Fournier-Pargoire; Albin-Michel,
Paris: November 1948; 235 pages, Fr. 240.
Manuscript
Manuscript, dated "1943--1944," in HRC.

A.9.   ELEPHANT AND CASTLE: A RECONSTRUCTION
First American Edition
Rinehart, New York: January 27, 1949; 658 pages, $3.75.
Canadian Edition
Clarke Irwin, Toronto: January 27, 1949; 658 pages, $3.75.
First English Edition
Cassell, London: April 26, 1949; 692 pages, 15/=.
Second English Edition
Duckworth, London: June 1969; 692 pages, 50/=.
Second American Edition
Greenwood Press, Westport, Connecticut: 1970; 658 pages,
$23.75.
Third English Edition
Zenith Books, London: 1985.
Swedish Translation
As Och Aldrig Mötas de Tva; Bonniers, Stockholm: 1950;
Kr.22.00.
French Translation
As L'Elephant à la Tour, by Jeanne Fournier-Pargoire;
Albin-Michel, Paris: February 1954; 640 pages, Fr. 990.

Manuscript
Manuscript, dated "1945/1948," in HRC.

A.10   JOURNEY WITH STRANGERS (RECOLLECTION OF A JOURNEY)
American Edition
Rinehart, New York: April 27, 1952; 431 pages, $4.00.
(Entitled Journey With Strangers.)
Canadian Edition
Clarke Irwin, Toronto: April 27, 1952; 431 pages, $4.75.
First English Edition
Cassell, London: October 23, 1952; 399 pages, 15/=.
(Entitled Recollection of a Journey.)
Second English Edition
White Lion, London: 1973; 399 pages, Ł1.95.
Third English Edition
Michael Joseph, London: February 2, 1981.
Fourth English Edition
Zenith Books, London: 1983; 399 pages, Ł2.95.
Abridgements
In Omnibook, XIV, ix (August 1952), 1-49; and in Montreal
Star (February 7, 1953).
Manuscript
Manuscript, dated "1945 and 1948-1951," in HRC.

A.11.   THE STEPMOTHER
American Edition
Rinehart, New York: August 19, 1955; 310 pages, $3.50.
(Book-of-the-Month Club Recommendation, August 1955.)
Canadian Edition
Clarke Irwin, Toronto: August 19, 1955; 310 pages, $3.50.
First English Edition
Cassell, London: September 8, 1955; 224 pages, 12/6d.
Second English Edition
Four Square, London: August 1962; 2/6d.
Third English Edition
White Lion. London: 1973; 222 pages, Ł1.95.
Fourth English Edition
Michael Joseph, London: 1983; 222 pages, Ł8.95.
Fifth English Edition
Zenith Books, London: August 1984.
German Translation
As Die Stiefmutter, by Ernst Sander; C. Bertelsmann Ver-
lag, Gütersloh: 1957; 314 pages, DM.11.00.
Dramatization
See below, M.143.
Manuscript
Manuscript, dated "1952-1954," in HRC.

A.12.   MARCH THE NINTH
American Edition
Rinehart, New York: October 28, 1957; 371 pages, $4.50.

Canadian Edition
> Clarke Irwin, Toronto: October 28, 1957; 371 pages, $4.50.

First English Edition
> Geoffrey Bles, London: November 4, 1957; 350 pages, 15/=.
>
> (Book Society Selection, November 1957.)

Second English Edition
> Fontana, London: May 1960; 3/6d.

Third English Edition
> Zenith Books, London: March 1984; 350 pages, Ł2.95.

German Translation
> As Der 9 Marz; Sigbert-Mohn-Verlag, Gütersloh: November 1959; 432 pages, DM.14.80.

Dramatization for Television
> See below, M.144.

Manuscript
> First draft of Chapters X/XIV in HRC; typescript of complete novel, originally titled "Number Twelve," dated "1955-1957," in HRC.

A.13. IMAGE OF MY FATHER (THE INHERITOR)
English Edition
> Geoffrey Bles, London: September 1961; 431 pages, 18/=.
> (Entitled Image of My Father; Book Society Recommendation, September 1961.)

American Edition
> Harper & Bros., New York: January 1962; 431 pages, $4.95.
> (Entitled The Inheritor; Book-of-the-Month Club Recommendation, January 1962.)

Canadian Edition
> Musson, Toronto: January 1962; 431 pages, $4.95.

Manuscripts
> Following manuscripts and typescripts are in HRC:
> (1) Earliest notes for the novel, 33 pages 4to. Plus typed letter, signed, 1958, from a lawyer friend, offering technical advice about 'caveats.'
> (2) Working Notes, approximately 390 pages.
> (3) Original Holograph Rough Draft Version, entitled "The Inheritor," 765 pages fcap. Last page bears author's note "Finished Nov. '60."
> (4) Later Holograph Version, entitled "The Inheritor," as sent for typing, 582 pages fcap. Dated "Bletchingley 1957-60."
> (5) Holograph Rough Draft of closing chapter, later version. 49 pages fcap. On verso of first leaf author has written "This bit finished 4 January 1961."
> (6) Later Holograph Version of closing chapter, 41 pages fcap.
> (7) Typescript, used as copy-text for Bles edition, 640

pages 4to. Deleted material on lower half of p. 587 represents opening of the rejected version of the closing chapter. Revised copy begins on p. 588. Blurb material marks first appearance of title Image of My Father.

A.14 A CHILD POSSESSED
First English Edition
   Geoffrey Bles, London: September 1964; 351 pages, 21/=.
American Edition
   Harper & Row, New York: January 27, 1965; 351 pages, $4.95.
   (Book-of-the-Month Club Recommendation, January 1965.)
Canadian Edition
   Longman's, Don Mills, Ontario: January 27, 1965; 351 pages, $5.75.
Second English Edition
   Hodder, London: December 1967; 5/=.
Third English Edition
   Michael Joseph, London: 1977; 351 pages, Ł5.00.
Fourth English Edition
   Zenith Books, London: March 10, 1983; 300 pages, Ł2.50.
Manuscripts
   Following manuscripts and typescripts are in MOHC:
   (1) Manuscript of first draft of novel, entitled "Eugenie," 648 pages fcap.
   (2) Fair copy of manuscript, entitled "A Child Possessed," 369 pages fcap.
   (3) Two copies of typescript, one of which was the setting copy, 471 pages 4to.

A.15. JOHANNA AT DAYBREAK
First English Edition
   Michael Joseph, London: April 28, 1969; 314 pages, 30/=.
American Edition
   Harper's, New York: September 24, 1969; 314 pages, $6.95.
   (Book-of-the-Month Club Recommendation, September 1969.)
Second English Edition
   Michael Joseph, London: 1981; 314 pages, Ł6.25.
Third English Edition
   Zenith Books, London: 1983; 314 pages, Ł2.95.
Manuscripts
   Following manuscripts and typescripts are in MOHC:
   (1) Manuscript of first draft of novel, entitled "No Fault of Mine," 607 pages fcap.
   (2) Fair copy of manuscript, entitled "Johanna: A Novel," 338 pages fcap.
   (3) Two copies of typescript, entitled "Johanna at Daybreak," one of which was the setting copy, 450 pages 4to.
   (4) Set of corrected page proofs of First English Edition.

A.16. ORIGINS OF CATHLEEN: A DIVERSION
First English Edition
Michael Joseph, London: September 6, 1971; 350 pages, Ł2.50.
Second English Edition
Zenith Books, London: 1984.
Dutch Translation
Was translated by T. Lau in 1972, but apparently never published.
Manuscripts
Following manuscripts and typescripts are in MOHC:
(1) Manuscript of first draft of novel, entitled "Novel XVI," 524 pages fcap.
(2) Fair copy of manuscript, entitled "Origins of Cathleen: A Diversion," 355 pages fcap.
(3) Two copies of typescript, one of which was the setting copy, 514 pages 4to.

A.17. RISING
First English Edition
Michael Joseph, London: September 6, 1976; 359 pages, Ł5.00.
Second English Edition
Penguin Books, Harmondsworth: March 1982; 359 pages, Ł2.95.
Manuscripts
Following manuscripts and typescripts are in MOHC:
(1) Manuscript of first draft, started on March 21, 1971, aboard ship returning from South America. This version ends "...constantly awaiting him," 727 pages fcap.
(2) Fair copy of manuscript, ending "was within his powers" (page 355 of First Edition), 495 pages fcap, plus son Jeremy's additions, marked "J1/J8," 8 pages 4to.
(3) Typescript, 639 pages 4to. Jeremy's additions have been deleted, so typescript ends at p. 636, "...constantly awaiting him." Pages 640 and 641 of typescript are Margaret Hutchinson's epilogue.

B. Short Stories

(i) Short Stories Published Individually
18. "Every Twenty Years"
19. "A Rendezvous for Mr Hopkins"
20. "Mr Harptop Rings the Bell"
21. "The Last Page"
22. "In The Dark"
23. "Last Voyage"

24. "The Quixotes"
25. "Slaves of Women"
26. "The Tramp With A Visiting Card"
27. "A Prison in France"
28. "Elosindi's Christmas"
29. "The Everyday Weekend"
30. "Go Between"
31. "Education in Blackmail"
32. "A Photograph of Mrs Austin"
33. "Siesta"
34. "Excursion to Norway: Commando in Action"
35. "Exhibit A"
36. "Crossroads"
37. "All in the Day"
38. "Common Tongue"
39. "Old English Custom"
40. "A Question of Value"
41. "A Woman of Simplicity"
42. "The End of Innocence"
43. "How I Rose To Be An Australian Shoeshine Boy"
44. "Duel at Mont Lipaux"
45. "Anniversary"

(ii) Edition of Selected Stories
46. "The Quixotes" and Other Stories: The Selected Short
     Stories of R.C. Hutchinson
(i) Short Stories Published Individually
B.18. "Every Twenty Years"
     First Published
          The Empire Review, 324 (January 1928), 61-67.
          (Author's name given as "Coryton Hutchinson.")
     Reprinted
          O'Brien, ed., The Best British Short Stories 1928 (Jona-
          than Cape, London: 1928; Dodd, Mead, New York: 1928);
          and in The Sunday Express (May 11, 1930), 7.
     German Translation
          Das Leben (Leipzig), VII, iii (September 1929), 5-14.
     Manuscripts
          Two manuscripts in MOHC: one, addressed "137 Walton
          Street, Oxford," 13 pages fcap; a second, from "Oriel
          College, Oxford," 12 pages fcap.

B.19. "A Rendezvous for Mr Hopkins"
     First Published
          English Review, XLVIII, ii (February 1929), 212-216.
     Broadcast
          Read by the author on BBC National Programme, 2.00 p.m.,
          Sunday August 1, 1937. Repeated on National Programme,
          10:45 a.m., Monday November 21, 1938.
     German Translation
          Neues Wiener Journal (September 29, 1929) and in Familien-

Wochenblatt (Zurich) (April 19, 1930).
Hungarian Translation
Pester Lloyd, Budapest: 1929.
Typescript
Typescript, 8 pages 4to, in MOHC.

B.20. "Mr Harptop Rings the Bell"
First Published
Manchester Guardian Weekly (December 29, 1929), 20.
(Runner-up in Ghost Story Competition.)
German Translation
Neues Wiener Journal (March 6, 1930).

B.21. "The Last Page"
The Bermondsey Book, VIII, ii (March-May 1930), 65-77.

B.22. "In The Dark"
English Review, L, v (May 1930), 635-639.

B.23. "Last Voyage"
Manchester Guardian (November 25, 1931), 18.

B.24. "The Quixotes"
English Review, LIV, i (January 1932), 51-60

B.25. "Slaves of Women"
Storyteller (February 1932), 701-708.

B.26. "The Tramp With A Visiting Card"
Saturday Review (March 5, 1932), 243-244.

B.27. "A Prison in France"
English Review, LV, iii (September 1932), 281-294.

B.28. "Elosindi's Christmas"
First Published
Snapdragon (Norwich Hospitals Annual) (1934), pp. 53-58.
Typescript
Typescript, 18 pages 4to, in MOHC.

B.29. "The Everyday Weekend"
Punch (May 6, 1936), 514.

B.30. "Go Between"
First Published
News Chronicle (September 21-25, 1936).
Reprinted
Natal Advertiser (November 23-27, 1936); Illustrated
Weekly of India (November 14-December 12, 1937); Bris-
bane Courier Mail (December 27-31, 1937).
Typescript
Typescript, 57 pages 4to, in MOHC.

B.31. "Education in Blackmail"
First Published
News Chronicle (February 22-26, 1937).
Reprinted
Brisbane Courier Mail (January 17-21, 1938); Auckland
Weekly News (December 14, 1938--January 11, 1939).

B.32. "A Photograph of Mrs Austin"
Broadcast
Read by the author on BBC National Programme, 10:30
p.m., October 11, 1938. Repeated on BBC Overseas Ser-
vice, 7:40 p.m., December 26, 1938.
Manuscript and Typescript
Manuscript, addressed "Birdlip, Gloucester," 28 pages
fcap, in MOHC. Typescript, 19 pages 4to, in MOHC.

B.33. "Siesta"
First Broadcast
Read by the author on BBC National Programme, 9:30 a.m.,
Monday August 31, 1939.
Read by Basil Ashmore on BBC, 11:00 a.m., Tuesday Janu-
ary 21, 1947. Repeated, November 1, 1960.
Typescript
Typescript, 10 pages 4to, in MOHC.

B.34. "Excursion to Norway: Commando in Action"
First Published
Atlantic Monthly (July 1942), 7-13.
Manuscript
Manuscript, 31 pages, and corrected copy of printed ver-
sion, with pencilled amendments by author, both in MOHC.

B.35. "Exhibit A"
First Published
Leonard Russell, ed., The Saturday Book: Seventh Year
(Hutchinson, London: 1947).
Manuscript
Manuscript, 24 pages 4to, in MOHC.

B.36. "Crossroads"
First Published
Leonard Russell, ed., The Saturday Book: Eighth Year
(Hutchinson, London: 1948).
Manuscript and Typescript
Manuscript, 17 pages fcap, and typescript, 20 pages 4to,
both in MOHC.

B.37. "All In The Day"
First Published
Lilliput (April 1953), 51-55.
First Reprint

John Pudney, ed., The Pick of Today's Short Stories,
Volume IV (Putnam, London: 1953).
Second Reprint
Dennis Pepper, ed., A Time To Fight (Nelson, London:
1978), pp. 47-53.
Manuscript
Manuscript, 9 pages fcap, in MOHC.

B.38. "Common Tongue"
First Published
Evening News (July 10, 1953).
Reprinted
Glasgow Evening Citizen (September 26, 1953).
Manuscript and Typescript
Manuscript, 10 pages fcap, and typescript, 7 pages 4to,
both in MOHC.

B.39. "Old English Custom"
First Published
Evening News (September 7, 1953).
Reprinted
Johannesburg Sunday Times (January 31, 1954).
Manuscript and Typescript
Manuscript, 11 pages fcap, and typescript, 10 pages 4to,
both in MOHC.

B.40. "A Question of Value"
First Published
Evening News (December 8, 1953).
Manuscript and Typescript
Manuscript, 10 pages fcap, and typescript, 7 pages 4to,
both in MOHC.

B.41. "A Woman of Simplicity"
First Published
She (February 1956), 23-27.
Manuscript and Typescript
Manuscript, 105 pages fcap, and typescript, 102 pages
4to, both in MOHC.

B.42. "The End of Innocence"
First Published
Housewife (June 1956), 50-51, 127, 129-130.
Manuscript and Typescript
Manuscript, 15 pages fcap, and typescript, 14 pages 4to,
both entitled "Everything Settled," in MOHC.

B.43. "How I Rose To Be An Australian Shoeshine Boy"
First Published
John Pudney, ed., The Pick of Today's Short Stories,
Vol. VII (Putnam, London: 1956).

Manuscript and Typescript
   Manuscript, 7 pages fcap, and typescript, 7 pages 4to,
   both in MOHC.

B.44. "Duel at Mont Lipaux"
First Published
   John Bull (February 8, 1958), 7-9, 31-32.
Manuscript and Typescript
   Manuscript, 20 pages fcap, and typescript, 21 pages 4to,
   both entitled "A Peculiar Engagement," in MOHC.

B.45. "Anniversary"
First Published
   Argosy (December 1965), 91-100.
Reprinted
   Douglas Rutherford, ed., Best Underworld Stories (Faber,
   London: 1969).
Manuscripts
   Two manuscripts, one of 17 pages fcap, and a later draft,
   13 pages fcap, in MOHC.

(ii) Edition of Selected Stories
B.46. "The Quixotes" and Other Stories: The Selected Short Stories
   of R.C. Hutchinson, edited by Robert Green (Carcanet Press,
   Manchester: June 30, 1984).
   (Contains Nos. B.18-28, 32, 34-38, 40, 42-45; and H.93, 102,
   107, 113.)

C. Military History

C.47. Paiforce: The Official Story of the Persia and Iraq Command,
   1941-1946
Published
   His Majesty's Stationery Office, London: January 28,
   1949; 137 pages, 5/=.
   (Published anonymously.)
Manuscript and Typescript
   Manuscript, dated "April-July 1945," in HRC; typescript,
   2 bound volumes of 303 pages, dated "Baghdad, April-
   July 1945," in MOHC.

D. Play

D.48. Last Train South
Production
St. Martin's Theatre, Shaftesbury Avenue, London: August 11-September 3, 1938. Three Acts. "The action occurs in the course of some twelve hours, in the winter of 1919-1920" in "the stationmaster's office at Pavlograd, South Russia." Produced by Basil Dean and J.B. Priestley. Directed by Basil Dean.

Cast

Fyodor	John Abbott
Gaskin	Aubrey Dexter
Domenov	Morland Graham
Captain Bolitsin	Alastair MacIntyre
Anya	Flora Robson
Old Woman	Barbara Gott
Paul	Peter Murray Hill
Countess Rostova	May Agate
Olga	Greta Gynt
General Zadolski	C.M. Hallard
Bulka	George Woodbridge
Grott	W.G. Manning

Stage Setting by Edward Carrick; Production Manager: Basil Dearden; Publicity: W. MacQueen Pope.
Typescripts
Typescripts, one of 138 pages 4to, and another of 144 pages 4to, in MOHC. Also typescript of a play entitled "The Barrier," probably an early version of "Last Train South," 162 pages 4to, in MOHC.

E. Articles, Reviews and Talks

(Asterisk indicates an item of most interest)

E.49. "To Commerce Via The University"
Nineteenth Century, CVI, 633 (November 1929), 661-671.

E.50 "A Trip to Oslo"
Eastern Daily Press (Norwich) (1929).

E.51. "The Six Bobber"
English Review, L, i (January 1930), 102-107.
(Essay about a rail journey from Norwich to London.)

E.52. "Cars of Yesterday: The Rocket Reviewed"
Punch, 4956 (May 20, 1936), 562-564.

E.53. "Old Boys' Day, 1937"
        The Monktonian, XXI, xii (July 1937), 618-620.
        (The novelist was a former pupil of Monkton Combe School.)

E.54. "Apostasy"
        Punch, 5069 (June 15, 1938), 648-649.
        (Typescript, 6 pages 4to, in MOHC.)

E.55. "Brimpsfield, Gloucestershire: A Brief Account of Its Queer
        Church and Curious History" (n.d., c.1938.)

*E.56. "How Long Should A Novel Be?"
        Swinton and Pendlebury Public Libraries Bulletin, XII, ii
        (May 1939), 5-7.
        (Novelist's defense of the long novel, written about the same
        time as Testament.)

E.57. "Open Letter from a Shaving Man to the Manager of His Sea-
        side Hotel"
        Punch, 5133 (August 23, 1939), 216.

E.58. "Aliens at Bow Street"
        Spectator, 5804 (September 23, 1939), 404-405.
        (The novelist's account of his experience of waiting at a Lon-
        don police station in the company of many European aliens.
        Manuscript, 7 pages, in MOHC.)

E.59. "Bag and Bowler Hat"
        First Published
            St. Martin's Review, 584 (October 1939), 454-457.
            (An essay on commercial travellers.)
        Reprinted
            As "Salesman, Diplomat, Clerk-on-Wheels," Synopsis, IV,
            iv (November 1939), 69-72.
        Manuscript
            Manuscript, 8 pages, in MOHC.

E.60. "Marriage Under Repair"
        St. Martin's Review, 590 (April 1940), 182-185.
        (Article on marriage-guidance, written with his sister, Marga-
        ret R. Hutchinson.)

*E.61. Untitled commentary on his own work in Stanley J. Kunitz
        and H. Haycraft, eds., Twentieth-Century Authors (H.W.
        Wilson, New York: 1942), pp. 696-697.

E.62. "G.W.F.R. Goodridge"
        The Monktonian, XXIII, ix (July 1944), 416-418.
        (Obituary of a celebrated schoolmaster. Manuscript, 5 pages,
        in MOHC.)

E.63.   "War Office Calling The Army"
        Talk broadcast on BBC General Forces Programme, 4:30 p.m.,
        Tuesday August 29, 1944. (On the Army Cadet Force.)

E.64.   "Old Monktonian Dinner"
        The Monktonian, XXIV, ii (April 1946), 94-97.

E.65.   Obituary of H.M. Grattan-Doyle
        The Times (January 8, 1947).

*E.66. "My Apologia"
        First Published
            John O'London's Weekly (April 15, 1949), 223.
        Reprinted
            As "If One Must Write Fiction," Saturday Review of Lit-
            erature, XXII, xxxvi (September 3, 1949), 6-7, 37.

E.67.   "South London"
        Sunday Times (February 5, 1950).
        (Review of S.P. Myers, London South of the River; written
        soon after Elephant and Castle.)

E.68.   "The Old Monktonian Dinner, 1950"
        The Monktonian, XXV, v (April 1951), 294-296.

*E.69. "My First Novel"
        Broadcast
            Broadcast on BBC Home Service, 11:15 a.m., Sunday
            March 29, 1953.
        Reprinted
            The Listener (April 2, 1953), 567-568.
        Manuscript and Typescript
            Manuscript, 16 pages fcap, and typescript in MOHC.

*E.70. "The Pace for Living"
        Broadcast
            Broadcast on BBC Home Service, 9:15 a.m., Sunday Sep-
            tember 6, 1953.
        First Reprint
            The Listener (September 17, 1953), 457-458.
        Second Reprint
            Vogue (March 1, 1954), 134, 172-173.
        Manuscript and Typescript
            Manuscript, 10 pages fcap, and typescript in MOHC.

*E.71. Untitled commentary on his own work in Stanley J. Kunitz,
        ed., Twentieth-Century Authors: First Supplement (H.W.
        Wilson, New York: 1955), p. 472.

*E.72. "Unfinished Novel"
        Talk broadcast on BBC Home Service, 3:00 p.m., Sunday

October 21, 1956, with extracts from the novel read by Carle-
ton Hobbs.
(Typescript, 11 pages fcap, in MOHC.)

E.73. "Who Was Theophilus?"
Merstham Review (December 1957), 5-6.
(Review of Canon Roger Lloyd, The Letters of Luke the
Physician.)

E.74. "Old Monktonian Dinner"
The Monktonian, XXVII, ii (April 1958), 110-112.

E.75. "The Stranded Clergyman"
Merstham Review (November 1958), 6-7.
(On the work of the Family Welfare Association. Manuscript,
3 pages, in MOHC.)

E.76. "Voice in Wilderness"
First Published
    The New Beacon (R.N.I.B.), XLIII, 505 (April 25, 1959),
    84-85.
    (On the experience of recording a technical book for the
    blind.)
Reprinted
    News Review (Central Council for the Care of Cripples)
    (Summer 1959), 17-18.
Manuscript
    Manuscript, 3 pages fcap, in MOHC.

*E.77. Untitled talk broadcast on BBC Home Service, November 19,
1960.
(On the danger of the blurb to a novel. Manuscript, 5 pages
fcap, in MOHC.)

E.78. "The Vehicle and The Book"
Broadcast on the BBC Home Service, 3:30 p.m., Sunday
February 26, 1961.
(On reading while travelling. Manuscript, 9 pages fcap, and
typescript in MOHC.)

E.79. "Freedom to Spend"
Broadcast on BBC Home Service, 9:10 a.m., April 19, 1961.
(Manuscript, 11 pages fcap, and typescript in MOHC.)

E.80. "On Useless Souvenirs"
Broadcast on BBC Home Service, 3:25 p.m., Sunday October
15, 1961.
(Manuscript, 11 pages fcap, and typescript in MOHC.)

*E.81. "Birth of A Child Possessed"
Mental Health, XXVI, i (Spring 1967), 26-27.
(Manuscript, 4 pages fcap, in MOHC.)

*E.82.   Essay on Ernest Raymond
         Camden Journal (December 1968).
         (Manuscript, entitled "The Work of Ernest Raymond: A Syn-
         optic View," 4 pages fcap, in MOHC.)

E.83.   "Schoolmaster Extraordinary"
         The Old Monktonian Gazette, II, xiv (November 1969), 442-
         444.
         (Review of A.F. Lace, My Own Trumpet. Manuscript, 4
         pages fcap, in MOHC.)

E.84.   "New and Vivid Experience"
         Surrey Mirror (November 19, 1971).
         (Review of R. Brownrigg, Who's Who in the New Testament.)

E.85.   "Graeme Hendrey, 1885-1972"
         Godstone Parish Magazine (July 1972), 4-5.
         (Obituary of the author's friend, the husband of the novelist,
         Eiluned Lewis.)

*E.86.   Untitled commentary on his work in James Vinson, ed., Con-
         temporary Novelists (St. James Press, London: 1972), p. 658.

E.87.   "Ernest Raymond"
         Royal Society of Literature Reports for 1973-1974, 1974-75,
         pp. 27-8.
         (Obituary. Manuscript, 3 pages fcap, in MOHC.)

F.   Letters

F.88.   Two Men of Letters: Correspondence Between R.C. Hutchin-
         son Novelist and Martyn Skinner Poet, 1957-1974, ed., Ru-
         pert Hart-Davis (Michael Joseph, London: 1979).

SECTION TWO: UNPUBLISHED MATERIAL

G. Novels

G.89. "The Hand of the Purple Idol"
(A juvenile thriller. Manuscript, undated, two notebooks, in MOHC.)

G.90. "The Caravan of Culture by Patricia Post"
(An epistolary novel of 31 chapters, the only novel Hutchinson called "a pot boiler," written about 1930; typescript, 386 pages 4to, in MOHC.)

H. Short Stories

(All are quarto typescripts unless indicated; all deposited in MOHC.)

H.91. "Adventurer Unsaluted" (4 pages).

H.92. "An Artist by Testament" (22 pages).

H.93. "At Grips With Morpheus" (14 pages).

H.94. "Black or White" (3 pages).

H.95. "The Conquest of Calpurnia" (10 pages).

H.96. "Courtesies of Commerce" (6 pages).

H.97. "Epilogue by the Stage Manager" (6 pages).

H.98. "Fog Off Flushing" (20 pages).

H.99. "Franziska" (Manuscript, 104 pages fcap).

H.100. "Going Begging" (5 pages).

H.101. "An Informal Call" (8 pages).

H.102.   "James Returns" (14 pages).

H.103.   "The Journey Begins" (16 pages).

H.104.   "Mens Sana" (17 pages).

H.105.   "No Wine for the Regular Guests" (5 pages).

H.106.   "November the 29th" (2 pages).

H.107.   "Outsiders: Three Sketches" (15 pages).

H.108.   "Penny Wise" (5 pages).

H.109.   "A Question of Identity" (4 pages).

H.110.   "A Scientist Dines" (9 pages).

H.111.   "A Sense of Proportion" (13 pages).

H.112.   "The Uneconomic Man" (8 pages).

H.113.   "The Wall Not Made With Hands" (16 pages).

H.114.   "The War Books and My Nephew" (13 pages).

H.115.   "The Way of Kindness" (31 pages).

H.116.   "The Wynforth Case" (27 pages).

I. Plays

    (All the items in this section are deposited in MOHC)

I.117.   "Dona Luisa: A Play in Three Acts by Ramon Barros"
         (Play set in Aragon, in the late summer of 1937. Address
         given as "Redhill." Manuscript, 22 pages fcap. Also an
         early draft, 134 pages fcap, and a typescript of same, 110
         pages 4to.)

I.118.   "The Daughters of Dr Humboldt: A Play in Three Acts by
         Franz Wien"
         (Play set in East Germany, March 1950. Address given as
         "Redhill." Manuscript, 34 pages fcap, with first draft and
         notes; also a corrected typescript of same, 50 pages 4to.
         This play was probably completed in October 1961, and then
         revised as "A Pattern of Daughters: A Play in Three Acts
         by Francis Fielding." There is a typescript, 52 pages 4to,
         of this revised version.)

I.119. "Mount Hercules: A Play in Three Acts"
(Play set in the lounge of the Auberge de la Dent d'Hercule,
Haute Savoie. Probably completed in May 1959. Typescript,
112 pages 4to.)

I.120. "Northern Star Or Oh Constancy!: A Play in Three Acts"
(Play set between 1927 and 1936, on board S.S. Tornessa,
in a London office, and in a house in Bristol. Typescript,
142 pages 4to, addressed from "Birdlip, Gloucester." Also
a later version, addressed from "Crondall, Farnham," typescript, 142 pages 4to.)

I.121. "Voyage in Twilight: A Play in Three Acts"
(Set in a convalescent home near Matlock, between the wars.
Typescript, 164 pages 4to.)

I.122. "Experiment with Madame de Chauvel: A Play in Three Acts"
(Set in Estwich Assize Court and in a Suffolk guest house.
Typescript, 118 pages 4to.)

I.123. "The Secret Bastion: A Play in Three Acts"
(Set in the Artists; Room of the Salisbury Concert Hall,
Nottingham, and in a hotel in Carlisle. Typescript, 154
pages 4to.)

I.124. "The Rest of Hake: A Farce in Three Acts by Coryton Ray"
(Set in 1957 in the Cornish studio of the late Washington
Hake. Typescript, addressed "Crondall, Farnham," 118
pages 4to. Also another version, entitled "Happy Return:
An Aesthetic Comedy in Three Acts by Coryton Ray.")

I.125. "The Circle"
(Synopsis of a short radio play; typescript, 3 pages 4to.)

J. Verse

J.126. "Shameless Behaviour at Barmouth"
(Humorous verse, 22 lines and title, probably intended for
Punch; typescript, 2 pages 4to, in MOHC.)

K. Translation

K.127. Translation of part of Scene Three of Anouilh's Le Voyageur
Sans Baggage.
(Manuscript, 28 pages fcap, in MOHC.)

L. Talks and Articles

(All the items in this section are deposited in MOHC.)

L.128. "Epic Flight"
(Humorous essay. Typescript, 9 pages 4to.)

L.129. "Guidance for Maidens"
(Humorous essay on Shaw's Intelligent Woman's Guide to Socialism and Capitalism (1928); typescript, 5 pages 4to.)

L.130. "Home of Lost Corpses"
(Humorous essay about a literary tour of Oxford; typescript, 4 pages 4to.)

L.131. "In Defence of Grub Street"
(Defense of the novel; typescript, 7 pages 4to.)

L.132. "It's a Way They Have in America"
(Humorous essay, typescript, 6 pages 4to.)

L.133. "A Little Out of Line"
(School reminiscences. Manuscript, 8 pages fcap, and typescript, 7 pages 4to.)

L.134. "More Science"
(Humorous essay about a science conference.)

L.135. "Motorists: Read This and Stop Worrying"
(Humorous essay on motor maintenance. Typescript, 5 pages 4to.)

L.136. "My Biggest Thrill"
(Humorous essay, typescript 4 pages 4to.)

L.137. "Nightmare Before Babylon"
(Visit to Babylon, 1945; designed as a radio talk.)

L.138. "No Business of Ours?"
(Review of Fr. Borrelli, Children of the Sun; manuscript, 2 pages fcap.)

L.139. "Our Business"
(Humorous essay on advertising; typescript, 5 pages 4to.)

L.140. "Postscript"
(An army exercise; designed as a radio broadcast; manuscript, 5 pages fcap.)

L.141. "Records for 1930"

(Humorous essay about the weather; typescript, 4 pages 4to.)

L.142. "Review of Iris Origo, A Measure of Love"
(Designed as a radio broadcast.)

M. Dramatizations by Other Writers

M.143. Hutchinson's novel, The Stepmother, was adapted for the
stage by Warren Chetham-Strode, and ran under the same
title at St. Martin's Theatre, London, from November 5 until November 29, 1958, almost exactly twenty years after the
appearance of his own play, Last Train South, at the same
theatre. Before its West End run, The Stepmother had toured
the provinces, receiving generally favorable reviews for the
players and for the script. The London production that followed also attracted good reviews for the actors, but Chetham-Strode's script was widely criticized. Miss Maggie
Smith, as Vere, was particularly well received. The Times
(November 6) found hers a "delightfully wristy performance,"
and it was felt that she was "well launched for a sparkling
career" (Oxford Mail, November 8). Doris Lessing, too, remarked that her part was "wonderfully played" (The Observer, November 9). After its brief run in the West End,
The Stepmother was played by several provincial repertory
companies, mostly in the south of England.
(Typescript of Chetham-Strode's adaptation, entitled "The
Image," in MOHC; the play was published by Samuel French,
London: 1959.)

M.144. The script for a three-act television adaptation of March The
Ninth was written by Elizabeth Lincoln for Associated Re-
diffusion Ltd. in January 1961, but was never broadcast.
(Typescript, 76 pages fcap, in MOHC.)

N. Letters

N.145. Letters from R.C. Hutchinson
HRC holds letters from Hutchinson to Hugh Walpole (1936,
1938); to PEN (1936-1939); and to Richard Church (1957-
1968). The novelist's letters to his wife, many written
during their wartime separation, are in MOHC.

N.146. Letters to R.C. Hutchinson

(A) Letters in HRC

HRC has a sizeable holding of letters to Hutchinson, the largest single collections being those from Richard Church, Sir Reader William Bullard, and from Robert Gittings.

N.147. Letters from Richard Church

Thirty Autograph letters, one with three manuscript poems, six typed letters, all signed. With carbon typescript, signed, of a further poem and the postscript from an autograph letter from Paul Scott to Church, forwarded to Hutchinson. Written from various addresses in Kent, 1957 and 1963-1971. Together ninety pages 8vo and 4to. One letter is addressed to Margaret, Hutchinson's wife.

An excellent group of letters, fully recording Church's long-held admiration for Hutchinson as a fellow craftsman, and providing much material of great biographical and critical interest. The first letter, in 1957, refers to the recent first meeting between the two men ("It was as though we had met after long acquaintance. Perhaps we are old soldiers together on our relative battlefields of words?").

The second letter, written in 1963, praises Hutchinson's Testament (first published in 1938), which Church had recently returned to in one of his Christian Science Monitor monthly articles, also published in Country Life (see below, S.418.) In his next letter he is deeply moved at Hutchinson's wish to dedicate his forthcoming novel, A Child Possessed, to him. Subsequent letters contain lengthy comments on it (Church reads it in proof form), particularly in the four-page letter of August 9, 1964. (Church reviewed the novel in Country Life: see below, S.490). Further encouragement and praise continues to the very last letter (December 7, 1971), which concerns Origins of Cathleen, which Church also reviewed (see below, S.501). Hutchinson, in turn, is the originator of the eventually successful plan for a volume of Church's poems in manuscript facsimile, much to the latter's delight (1966). The three fair copies of poems sent with his letter of July 30, 1966, were written shortly after his first wife's death. The carbon typescript poem accompanied his last letter and is a verse tribute to Andrew Young, written on the announcement of Young's death in 1971. Attached to the letter of October 14, 1964, is the Postscript (initialled "P") from Paul Scott's letter to Church. It relates Scott's early admiration for Hutchinson when serving in the same regiment in World War II (and see below, N.312).

This collection also contains the Introduction Church wrote for the 1968 edition of Hutchinson's Shining Scabbard (see above, A.5.4). Carbon typescript, revised, with 12

words inserted or substituted in Church's hand. Signed.
9 pages La. 4to. (Originally sent with Church's letter of
November 14, 1967.)

N.148. Letters from Sir Reader William Bullard
1885-1976. Minister, later Ambassador. Tehran (Persia),
1939-1946; Director of Institute of Colonial Studies, Oxford,
1951-1956. Author of Britain and the Middle East and of an
autobiography, The Camels Must Go (1961).

Eleven autograph letters, twenty typed letters (many
with extensive autograph material added) and three autograph correspondence cards, all signed or initialled. Oxford, 1962-1974. Together 49 pages 4to and 8vo. With en-
closures, being (1) carbon typescript transcript of an account of a séance at Oxford, c. 1916; (2) photocopy of a
Wrong Box Society Dinner at the Athenaeum Club. These
are discussed in letters of 1971 and 1966 respectively.

Hutchinson had first met Sir Reader in Tehran when
he was writing Paiforce His letters to the novelist display
his warm interest in Hutchinson's works and in his family.

N.149. Letters from Richard Gittings
Eleven autograph letters, one typed letter, all signed. (One
addressed to Mrs. Margaret Hutchinson.) 1963-1969 and
1975. Together 15 pages 4to and 8vo. With 9 Christmas
cards.

Cordial letters, addressed "Dear Ray." The first an-
nounces Gittings' resignation from the B.B.C. to embark
upon his great biographical and critical study of Keats. Subsequent letters concern progress on this and other works.
Gittings writes of his pleasure in his American tours, of his
admiration of Hutchinson's work, and his pleasure that A
Child Possessed brought Hutchinson a prize.

N.150. Other Letters in HRC
HRC also contains a number of single letters and short
series.

N.151. Ackland, Rodney
Two typed letters, signed. 1946-1948. Promising and later
sending the script of his play Crime and Punishment.

N.152. Bowen, Elizabeth
One autograph letter and one typed letter, both signed.
1944 and 1964. Concerning Bowen's Court and The Little
Girls.

N.153. Cary, Joyce
Autograph letter, signed. 1948. 2 pages. About The
Horse's Mouth.

N.154. Crankshaw, Edward
Autograph letter, signed. 1972. 2 pages. An account, via
friends, of Richard Church's death, written some five days
afterwards.

N.155. Compton-Burnett, Ivy
Autograph postcard, signed. 1957.

N.156. Forester, C.S.
Typed letter, signed. New York, 1941. On "British Information Services" stationery. Suggesting that Hutchinson
write an account of his personal military experiences, or a
novel, "from the point of view of this office" (i.e., for
propaganda). "The sort of thing that I have in mind would
do the work that The First Hundred Thousand did in the last
war--although I have no doubt that whatever you wrote
would be far better as Literature ... I have always been an
admirer of your work, and have more than once publicly declared myself so in reviews in the American press...."
(Forester had reviewed The Fire and The Wood in New York
in 1940: see below, S.430.) (His suggestion may well have
inspired Hutchinson to write a short story about the war in
Norway, published in Atlantic Monthly in 1942 as "Excursion
to Norway": see above, B.34.)

N.157. Gibbs, Philip
Two autograph letters, signed. 1933. Praising Hutchinson's
The Unforgotten Prisoner.

N.158. Hart-Davis, Rupert
Three autograph letters, signed, one typed letter, signed.
1955-1969. Together 7 pages. Praising The Stepmother
and "hoping against hope" that he might be the publisher of
Hutchinson's next novel; later writing of March The Ninth
and Johanna at Daybreak. (See below, N.264.)

N.159. Hartley, L.P.
Autograph letter, signed. 1963. 3 pages. Acknowledging
Hutchinson's praise, with reflections on the English reading
public: "... The romance, and imagination, and strange-
ness which you, for instance, put into your novels, don't
find a response ... from our materialistic generation."

N.160. Hobson, Harold
One autograph letter and one typed letter, both signed.
1949 and 1974. Together 3 pages. "... Richard Church and
I did our best to get it (Elephant and Castle) the Sunday
Times £1,000 book prize, and at one time it looked as though
we should succeed..." (1949). The two-page autograph let-
ter of 1974 (when Hobson was elected to the Fellowship of
Oriel College) recalls "so many happy memories of conversa-

tions in the Great Quad," and lists Hutchinson, A.J.P. Taylor and J.I.M. Stewart as "others who deserve" to be elected Fellows.

N.161. Hughes, Richard
Typed letter, signed. Merioneth, 1970. Includes comparison of Hutchinson's generation at Oxford with his own, concluding "Do you ever go back now? After my Double Fourth I didn't dare until I had children of my own to visit there."

N.162. Lawrence, Geoffrey (later Lord Oakley)
Autograph letter, signed. Nurnberg, nd. (c.1945). As a "great admirer" of Hutchinson's work, he invites him to attend the Nuremberg Trials. (Hutchinson accepted the invitation.)

N.163. Macaulay, Rose
Autograph letter, signed. 1956. 2 pages. Regarding an unnamed book, almost certainly The Towers of Trebizond, writes "... the book was a cri de coeur wrapped up in a few jokes, and you received both...."

N.164. Paton, Alan
Autograph letter, signed. Natal, South Africa, 1949. Closely written on an air-letter form. "... Since I left the Diepkloof Reformatory I have settled to a life ... of writing...." Praises Testament, which a mutual friend had sent him from London.

N.165. Phelps, William Lyon
Three autograph letters, signed. To Mrs. Hutchinson. New Haven and elsewhere, May-July 1940. 10 pages. Warmly enthusiastic letters regarding American publication of one of Hutchinson's novels. "My faith in him, which began in 1928 with The Answering Glory has steadily increased."

N.166. Sansom, William
Autograph letter, signed. 1974. 2 pages. Thanks Hutchinson for "kind words" (about The World of Marcel Proust) and recommends highly Howard Moss' The Magic Lantern of Marcel Proust.

N.167. Taylor, Elizabeth
Autograph letter, signed. 1972. "... so glad that you liked Mrs Palfrey; and the things you had to say about it pleased me very much, & encouraged me."

N.168. Thomas, Helen
Widow of Edward Thomas. Typed letter, signed. Thanks Hutchinson for "appreciation and understanding" of her book, adding "Just before I became blind I made a record of some of Edward's poems, which I gather you know and love...."

N.169.   West, Rebecca
Autograph letter, signed. 1967. "... I liked Testament
and Elephant and Castle to the point of suddenly speaking
about them in speeches which were supposed to be on another subject--I just felt that it was better for everybody,
including me, that it should be so." (In a footnote she adds
"Twice this happened.")

N.170.   Zweig, Stefan
Two autograph letters, signed. In English. 1939. 3 pages.
"I wrote a dozen of letters on behalf of your book (Testament) to my American and other foreign publishers." Men-
tions Otto Zapek (see below, N.171.)

N.171.   Cape, Jonathan
Two typed letters, signed. With copy of a letter from Otto
Zapek to Cape. 1940. 3 pages 4to. "I have agreed to publish Mr Otto Zapek's autobiography ... he speaks of staying
with you at Farnham when war was declared...."

N.172.   Flower, Newman
Managing director of Cassell's, publishers of Hutchinson's
novels for much of his career. Three autograph letters,
signed. 1938-1940. Together 7 pages 4to and 8vo. The
first, May 16, 1938, on Cassell's stationery, is his ecstatic
reaction after a first reading of Testament: "... certainly
one of the very finest novels that has come to Cassell's during my 32 years here. The concluding part is simply magnificent ... I do not feel that the book should be cut."
After promising to send "figures" later, he advises: "Do
not think of abandoning novel-writing.... You have done
splendid spade-work, and a knowledge of your quality is
getting through the literary world. You are going on to
very big sales...." The second, October 22, 1938, (after
Testament had been published), "... But you owe me nothing; all that has come to you, your own genius has brought
to you." Recounting his close following of Hutchinson's
career since his first novel, Flower concludes: "Meanwhile
best thanks to you for your letter. It was worth while being
in the publishing world for so many years to get a letter
like that." The third letter praises Hutchinson's subsequent
novel, The Fire and the Wood.

N.173.   Other Correspondents Are:

N.174.   May Agate
N.175.   John Arlott
N.176.   Faith Baldwin
N.177.   Jacques Barzun
N.178.   Marc Boxer (the cartoonist "Marc")
N.179.   D. Clayton Calthrop

N.180. Fr. M.C. D'Arcy, S.J. (2)
N.181. Ruth Draper
N.182. Leonora Eyles
N.183. André Van Guyseghem
N.184. G. Rostrevor Hamilton
N.185. A.P. Herbert
N.186. Michael Holroyd
N.187. Trevor Huddleston (in 1967, when Bishop of Masasi, Tan-
        zania)
N.188. Derek Hudson
N.189. Garry Hogg
N.190. Christopher Hollis
N.191. Admiral Sir William James
N.192. Storm Jameson (2 autograph letters, 4 typed letters, all
        signed)
N.193. Elizabeth Jenkins
N.194. Eric Linklater (autograph letter, signed. 4 pages)
N.195. S.P.B. Mais (2)
N.196. Robert Morley
N.197. Herman Ould
N.198. Eric Partridge
N.199. Cyril Ray
N.200. Ernest Raymond
N.201. Flora Robson
N.202. Edward Sackville-West
N.203. General Sir Arthur Smith (G.O.C. Paiforce. 1949. On re-
        ceiving Paiforce: "... you did magnificently in getting the
        authorities to agree to even this shortened form. For all I
        know they are right in saying that the last part had to be
        condensed.")
N.204. L.A.G. Strong
N.205. Wilfrid Thesiger
N.206. H.M. Tomlinson
N.207. Philip Toynbee
N.208. Irving Wardle
N.209. E.B. White (of The New Yorker. "... glad to have your
        note approving the Strunk book...")
N.210. Emlyn Williams

        (B) Letters in MOHC
        MOHC has a large number of letters from 'fans,' the great
        majority from unknown admirers, several anonymous. It
        also contains letters from the following correspondents (ar-
        ranged in chronological order):

N.211. Phelps, William Lyon
        Emeritus Professor of English Literature, Yale University.
        June 7, 1932. Savoy Hotel, London. Congratulates Hutchin-
        son on The Answering Glory: "magnificent in characteriza-
        tion, and inspiring."

N.212. Day Lewis, C.
One of the editors of Orion. November 6, (?1933). Invites
a contribution from Hutchinson for the second issue of
Orion: "we are very eager to print some of your work."

N.213. Flower, Newman
Managing director, Cassell's. January 1, 1934. Reports
sales to date of The Unforgotten Prisoner as 15,000 copies.
Quotes Compton Mackenzie's description of Agate's Express
review (see below, S.373.) as "scandalous." "Tell the
young man from me that I wrote what I did with complete
sincerity, and give him my congratulations."

N.214. Farrar, John
Farrar and Rinehart, 232 Madison Avenue, New York.
February 14, 1935. Quotes several favorable reactions to
One Light Burning, including a letter from Stephen Vincent
Benet: "R.C. Hutchinson is somebody with real imagination
and a fine gift of excitement. After all the tidy, neat novels, it's a pleasure to read a book that spills over with its
own abundance--and a book where the world the author creates is so entirely his own."

N.215. Dobrée, Bonamy
Mendham Priory, Harleston, Norfolk. February 22, 1935.
Impressed by One Light Burning and asks if he could meet
Hutchinson in Norwich one day. (Hutchinson was at that
time resident in Norwich.)

N.216. Phelps, William Lyon
Yale University. February 23, 1935. Expresses "immense
delight" over One Light Burning: "Somehow you combine
wit and spirituality: and both are needed."

N.217. Sackville-West, Edward
Knole, Sevenoaks. March 2 (?1935). Expresses admiration
for One Light Burning, which shows that Hutchinson has
"become one of the few important English novelists writing
now." Impressed by Hutchinson's interest in method, and
defends the novel's obliqueness against reviewers' criticism.
Also inquires meaning of 'marijuana'; and whether Hutchinson was particularly interested in de Quincey, of whom
Sackville-West was then writing a biography (published in
1936).

N.218. Walpole, Hugh
Brackenbury, Manesty Park, Keswick. April 16, 1936 (?may-
be September or October). "Dear Mr Hutchinson,/ I'm writing only a line to say how glad I am that the reviewers have
had the sense to see how grand a book Shining Scabbard is.
I was responsible for the Book Society choice of your first

novel and so I feel avuncular to you. Probably you'll think
that cheek but in any case I'm as pleased as Punch at your
success./ Yours sincerely,/ Hugh Walpole."

N.219. **Higham, David**
Director of Pearn, Pollinger and Higham, Literary Agents,
6 Norfolk Street, Strand, London. September 22, 1936.
"Dear Mr Hutchinson,/ I must congratulate you on the magnificent reception The Shining Scabbard is getting. And
what a good show Cassells are giving it. I do hope it justi-
fies everything. I believe it will./ Yours,/ David Higham."

N.220. **Farrar, John**
Telegram. October 20, 1936. Announcing selection of Shining Scabbard by United States Book-of-the-Month Club, and
possible sale of up to 50,000 copies.

N.221. **Collins, Alan C.**
Manager, New York office, Curtis Brown Ltd., 18 East 48th
Street. November 17, 1936. Congratulates Hutchinson on
BOMC selection of Shining Scabbard, and expresses surprise
that he had never visited France. "It is incomprehensible
to me that anyone could do Shining Scabbard without an intimate knowledge of the French family point of view, for when
I read the book, I felt certain that you knew the French and
their ways thru long association."

N.222. **Emmanuel, L. Miss**
The To-Morrow Club, 34 Campden Hill Gardens, London W8.
November 18, 1936. Invites Hutchinson to speak to the club
at 8:10 p.m. on Thursday, February 18, 1937.

N.223. **Agate, May**
Actress who played "Countess Rostova" in Last Train South.
11 Elms Crescent, London SW4. August 12, 1938. Thanks
Hutchinson for his flowers and charming letter. Consoles
him on press notices of Last Train South, and notes that he
"could not stand against the demands of (his) producer."

N.224. **Dexter, Aubrey**
Actor who played "Gaskin" in Last Train South. 158 Ebury
Street, London SW1. August 12, 1938. Thanks Hutchinson
for his charming letter and consoles him for hostile reviews.
Believes that the reconstruction of the play by Basil Dean
unbalanced it, and implies that the message about hatred had
been added to Hutchinson's original script.

N.225. **Robson, Flora**
37 Downshire Hill, London NW3. August 13 (1938). Thanks
Hutchinson for flowers and charming letter sent on the first
night. Consoles him for bad reviews and blames failure of

Last Train South on the miscasting of the "General." Thinks
that with the departure of Basil Dean all the actors will im-
prove enormously and recommends that Hutchinson send his
next play to Tyrone Guthrie. "He is no good with Shake-
speare, but your writing is just his stuff." Sends love and
respects from the whole cast. Signed "Yours very sincerely,/
Flora Robson."

N.226. Walpole, Hugh
90, Piccadilly, London W1. August 14, 1938. Criticizes
Last Train South for lacking a clash between Whites and
Reds in Act Three, and Dean's production for being noisy
and melodramatic. Remarks that Hutchinson has a "true gift"
for the theatre and hopes that he won't drop it.

N.227. Gott, Barbara
Actress who played "Old Woman." 408 Duncan House, Dol-
phin Square, London SW1. August 14, 1938. Thanks
Hutchinson for flowers and kind letter.

N.228. Abbott, John
Actor who played "Fyodor." 12 Manchester Square, London
W1. Undated. Consoles Hutchinson for hostile notices.

N.229. Dean, Basil
Little Easton Manor, Dunmow, Essex. August 14, 1938.
"Most grieved" at the critical reception of Last Train South.
Expresses "eager anticipation" of the next play.

N.230. Curtis Brown, Spencer
August 16, 1938. Dean and Priestley, the co-producers, had
altered Hutchinson's original script which writer felt had
harmed Last Train South. Criticizes Dean's production as
well, "with its attempts to whip the characters into drama."
The original script had been sent to New York for appraisal
there.

N.231. Priestley, J.B.
Billingham Manor, Isle of Wight. August 16, 1938. Offers
encouragement and consolation after the hostile press comments on Last Train South. Regrets the play hadn't had a
week's try-out before opening so that faults could have been
ironed out. "I believe you have a real talent and feeling for
the theatre, and I hope this experience will not keep you
out of it, for it needs people of your sort very badly, though
you'd never think so from the critics. I felt genuinely indignant, not as one of your managers, but as a fellow dramatist, at the way in which not one of them even gave you a
welcome into the Theatre. But we've all been through it./
With best wishes,/ Yours ever,/ J.B. Priestley."

N.232. Gynt, Greta
        Actress who played "Olga." Palace Gate House, Palace Gate,
        London W8. August 20, 1938. Thanks Hutchinson for his
        flowers and kind letter.

N.233. Carrick, Edward
        Set designer. 14, Soho Square, London W1. August 22,
        1938. Thanks Hutchinson for his letter and kind comments
        about the set, which Basil Dean had apparently altered "at
        the last moment."

N.234. Sackville-West, Edward
        Knole, Sevenoaks, Kent. August 25 (1938). Appalled by
        the stage clichés with which, he assumes, Dean and Priest-
        ley had stuffed the script. Last Train South is a good
        story and is at least a play "about something." Urges
        Hutchinson to be much firmer with his next producer and
        "refuse to let him cheapen your play for you."

N.235. Robson, Flora
        37 Downshire Hill, London NW3. September 3 (1938). Thanks
        Hutchinson for sending a copy of Testament. Now believes
        that she herself spoilt Last Train South by having sat quiet-
        ly for so long. Says that the cast is playing better now and
        the audience is more attentive. Wishes Testament a big suc-
        cess and says she will take it with her on holiday to the
        Scillies "tomorrow." Inquires for the children's whooping
        cough. "Very best wishes,/ Yours sincerely,/ Flora Rob-
        son."

N.236. Dexter, Aubrey
        158 Ebury Street, London SW1. September 4, 1938. Thanks
        Hutchinson for sending a copy of Testament and congratulates
        him on its fine reviews.

N.237. Sackville-West, Edward
        Knole, Sevenoaks, Kent. October 12 (1938). Extremely im-
        pressed with Testament and proud to be the novel's dedi-
        catee.

N.238. Hobson, Harold
        Christian Science Monitor, London SW1. October 17, 1938.
        Congratulates Hutchinson on the last act of Last Train South,
        a "really civilized play." Hopes he will continue to write for
        the theatre.

N.239. Sackville-West, Edward
        Knole, Sevenoaks, Kent. November 16 (1938). Informs
        Hutchinson that he had recommended Testament to Desmond Mc-
        Carthy, who was looking for a novel to put forward for The
        Sunday Times medal for fiction. David Garnett had told

Sackville-West that Constance, his mother, "much admires" the novel.

N.240.   **Evans, A. Dwye**
Director, Heinemann Ltd., 99 Great Russell Street, London WC1. March 29, 1939. Asks permission to quote Hutchinson's praise of Charles Kaufman's novel, Fiesta in Manhattan, of which Heinemann had recently bought English rights.

N.241.   **Raymond, Ernest**
Norton Lees, Hayward's Heath, Sussex. October 4, 1939. Offers to try to secure Hutchinson something in the Army other than "an ordinary infantry commission."

N.242.   **Raymond, Ernest**
Norton Lees, Hayward's Heath, Sussex. February 28, 1940. Hopes that Hutchinson's military service will enable him to write a big war novel and urges him to keep a diary, as Raymond had done at Gallipoli. Offers to help see The Fire and The Wood through the press if Hutchinson is prevented from doing so by military service.

N.243.   **Greene, S. Grafton**
Overseas Features Editor, Ministry of Information, Malet Street, London WC1. July 9, 1942. Encloses check for $250 received from Atlantic Monthly for Hutchinson's story "Excursion to Norway." Edward Weekes, Atlantic editor, is quoted as saying about the story: "... the very narrative I have been hungering for for months. The intricacy of the raid, the character of the men who undertook it and the authenticity of what they did, have all been set down without a shadow of doubt. It is a brilliant piece of writing and one which I am very proud to have in the Atlantic this summer."

N.244.   **Flower, Sir Newman**
Director, Cassell's, 210 High Holborn, London WC1. August 17, 1942. Reports that J.B. Priestley agreed with Flower's estimate of Hutchinson as "the finest novelist of our time." "J.B.P. has a great opinion of himself, but I think he has a greater opinion of you!" Continues: "The terrible thing to me is that the paper shortage has prohibited our reprinting Testament. I could have sold 200,000 now, if the Govt. would give us the paper. We have made special overtures to the Govt. on account of this book. But they won't budge an inch, even for the P.M.'s (Churchill's) new book which we are going to publish."

N.245.   **Sackville-West, Edward**
BBC, London W1. October 21, 1942. "My cousin, V. Sackville-West, has been reading 'Testament' with enthusiasm (she did not know your work before) and asked me about you."

N.246. Fraser, Robert
        Publications Division, Ministry of Information, Russell Square,
        London WC1, July 16, 1943. Invites Hutchinson to contrib-
        ute "material which goes beyond the ordinary limits of propa-
        ganda" to a weekly newspaper, published in Moscow, called
        "The British Ally."

N.247. Flower, Sir Newman
        Director, Cassell's. August 2, 1944. Admires Interim, "a
        brilliant piece of writing," but predicts that it won't be as
        popular as some of the other novels "because there is not
        so much 'story' in Interim."

N.248. Curtis Brown, Jean
        Literary Agents, 6 Henrietta Street, London WC2. Decem-
        ber 12, 1944. Informs Hutchinson that V. Sackville-West
        broadcast a talk on his work in the French Service of the
        BBC "last Wednesday."

N.249. Sackville-West, Edward
        Literary Editor, New Statesman. 20 Chester Square, Lon-
        don SW1. April 17, 1945. Apologizes for Philip Toynbee's
        "dreadful" review of Interim.

N.250. Hampden, John
        Publications Department, British Council, 3 Hanover Street,
        London W1. December 14, 1945. Invites Hutchinson to
        write a brochure on "The British Army," of about 12,000
        words, and offers 60 guineas for the copyright.

N.251. Flower, Sir Newman
        Director, Cassell's, 41 Castlemaine Avenue, South Croydon.
        December 20, 1945. Offers to supply Hutchinson with paper
        on which to write his next novel (Elephant and Castle) as
        Hutchinson had told him "yesterday" that he was so short
        of paper that he would have to write on the back of his
        earlier manuscripts. Describes him as "the most modest au-
        thor I've ever known in 40 years of publishing."

N.252. Sackville-West, V.
        Sissinghurst Castle, Kent. February 10, 1948. "Dear Mr
        Hutchinson,/ I hope you will forgive me for bothering you
        but I know that you are a friend of my cousin Eddie so I
        feel that I have some right to ask you a question which,
        after all, is in your own interests./ I am just about to
        go on a lecture tour in North Africa for the British Council,
        and propose to talk about some of your novels but I cannot
        for the life of me remember the title of the book you wrote
        about a French provincial town [Shining Scabbard]. There
        is something odd in my mind which can never register the
        titles of your books, greatly as I admire them. Could you

possibly send me a post card by return reminding me of
what this book was called, and could you also tell me if any
of your books have been translated into French?/ Yours sincerely,/ V. Sackville-West."

N.253. Luckham, Violet
Actress. 41 Belmont Street, Southport. June 7, 1949.
Congratulates Hutchinson on Elephant and Castle, and recalls reading his play in Spring 1941 ("O Constancy"). He
had sent the script to Violet and Cyril Luckham for their
criticism.

N.254. Luckham, Cyril and Violet
7b, Broadlands Road, Highgate, London N6. November 22,
1952. They had been fans of Hutchinson's since 1940, and
had both been deeply impressed with Recollection of a Journey.

N.255. Jameson, Margaret Storm
12 North Hill Court, Leeds 6. November 27, 1952. Describes Recollection of a Journey as "a magnificent novel,"
"a noble book."

N.256. Sackville-West, Edward
Long Crichel House, Wimborne. November 30, 1952. In the
middle of reading Recollection of a Journey, which he thinks
is Hutchinson's best novel since Shining Scabbard.

N.257. Broncel, Z.A.
312 Finchley Road, London NW3. March 17, 1953. Broncel
had been asked to translate a chapter from Recollection of
a Journey to be read at a meeting of the Union of Polish
Writers Abroad on March 24. Earlier, on February 8, 1953,
Broncel had produced a program on the novel, transmitted
on the BBC Polish Service. This aroused great interest
among Polish listeners and in the Polish emigré press.
Hutchinson did not attend the meeting of the UPWA, but did
send a letter of greetings to the Polish writers, to which
the meeting responded with a motion "of admiration and gratitude." (Letter from S. Stronski, Chairman, UPWA, March
27, 1953.)

N.258. Skinner, Pauline
Wife of poet, Martyn. Ipsden, Oxford. April 10, 1953.
Grateful that she had read Recollection of a Journey and
congratulates Hutchinson. It left her "gloriously inspired
and deeply comforted."

N.259. Skinner, Martyn
Poet. Ipsden, Oxford. April 11, 1953. Grateful that "there
is still someone writing who can navigate the novel under full
sail."

N.260. Broncel, Z.A.
312 Finchley Road, London NW3. April 21, 1953. Broncel
had sent the translation of Chapter XIX of Recollection of a
Journey (presumably the chapter read at the UPWA meeting
in March). Now he says that he has been approached by a
Polish Catholic emigré weekly, Zycie ("Life") for a translation from Recollection to appear in an issue devoted to the
fate of Poles in Russia. Broncel suggests a portion of the
chapter describing the deportation by train, and asks for
Hutchinson's approval.

N.261. Leitgeber, Witold
70 Talgarth Road, London W14. June 3, 1953. The writer
had given a 12-minute talk on the BBC Polish Service on
February 5, 1953, in which he praised Recollection of a
Journey.

N.262. Hough, Graham
Christ's College, Cambridge. February 9, 1955. Thanks
Hutchinson for his kind note about Hough's broadcasts. "I
have admired Testament for many years."

N.263. Hutchinson, Ann
23 Rosary Gardens, London SW7. July 25 (1956). Thanks
her father for the dedication of The Stepmother.

N.264. Hart-Davis, Rupert
36 Soho Square, London W1. August 19 and 26, 1955.
Writer had heard that Hutchinson might be leaving Cassell's
and asks if he might be allowed to publish him, since "for
more than twenty years I have thought of you as the greatest living novelist" and "a great imaginative writer." In the
second letter he thanks Hutchinson for his "delightful" re-
ply and says that he will "wait patiently, still nursing the
unconquerable hope that one day I shall have the honour
and joy of being your publisher."

N.265. Roberts, Denys Kilham
Secretary-General, The Society of Authors. 84 Drayton
Gardens, London SW10. November 9, 1955. Invites Hutchin-
son to sign the letter to The Times about the forthcoming
Copyright Bill.

N.266. Hill, Norah
Meadowsweet, Crondall, Farnham. December 4, 1956. Quotes
from letter she had received from Winifred Gerin. "Recently
I read one of my favourite R.C. Hutchinson's newer novels,
'Recollection of a Journey,' which, like all his others, I
thought wholly admirable. He is a great man--so penetrating
of the human heart and so feeling for this century's predicament. He stands alone among English writers for his deep

understanding of the continental soul--one might indeed say
of the universal soul. I have been reading quite a lot of
our best contemporary writers--C.P. Snow, Elizabeth Bowen,
etc. and fine as they are, they all seem so limited when compared to R.C. Hutchinson. If you ever do have an opportunity of meeting him, do tell him he has an unknown admirer of his work."

N.267. Cormack, M. Grant, Miss
Secretary, Belfast Centre, Irish P.E.N. 37 Castlereagh
Place, Belfast. January 15, 1958. Invites Hutchinson to
talk to the Belfast P.E.N. (He went in 1959.)

N.268. Reid, Kate
Actress. The White House Hotel, Hull. Undated (?October
1958.) Thanks Hutchinson for the encouragement he had
given her as an actress (in the dramatization of The Stepmother), and for sending her a copy of the novel. "Your
encouragement has meant more than anything else to me."

N.269. Todorovic, Zika
Editor, Politika. 35, Makedonska, Belgrade, Yugoslavia.
October 7, 1958. Invites Hutchinson to contribute to "a col-
lection of statements by contemporary writers."

N.270. Raymond, Ernest
22 The Pryors, East Heath Road, London NW3. October 27,
1958. Thanks Hutchinson for his kind comments about Raymond's latest novel, about Gallipoli.

N.271. Hunter, Ian
Actor. 113a Jermyn Street, London SW1. "Saturday."
(?November 1, 1958) Thanks Hutchinson for his "wonderful letter" and encouragement. (Hunter played the lead in
the dramatization of The Stepmother.)

N.272. Holland, Anthony
Designer. 6a Sloane Square, London SW1. November 8,
1958. Thanks Hutchinson "for all the nice things you said
about the sets" of The Stepmother.

N.273. Leach, E.A.
Secretary, The Association of Yorkshire Bookmen. January
5, 1960. Invites Hutchinson to address the Association.

N.274. Townend, Paul
Novelist. Hotel Waldheim, Obwalden, Switzerland. January
14, 1960. Asks for permission to quote Hutchinson's praise
of his previous thriller, Died O'Wednesday, on the jacket of
his forthcoming book.

N.275. Mattingley, Garrett
        308 West 104th Street, New York 25. January 22, 1960.
        Thanks Hutchinson for his letter of praise for Mattingley's
        book.

N.276. Wall, Bernard
        57 Ladbroke Road, London W11. February 17, 1960. Thanks
        Hutchinson for his letter of appreciation of his translation of
        Teilhard's The Phenomenon of Man (1959).

N.277. Sackville-West, Edward
        Long Crichel House, Wimborne. December 29, 1960. "I am
        sorry to hear that you are not satisfied with your new novel
        (Image of My Father), but you must not allow the antics of
        the young redbricks to get you down."

N.278. Church, Richard
        The Oast House, Curtisden Green, Cranbrook, Kent. Octo-
        tober 25, 1961. "This novel (Image of My Father) builds up
        with the power which is now characteristic of your work.
        Every phrase tells, and the ramifications of character into
        conduct, with the resultant drama, are worked out with an
        inevitability as subtle and as mysterious as events in real
        life."

N.279. Devins, Joseph H., Jr.
        US Army Language School, Presidio of Monterey, California.
        April 1, 1962. Writer working on an account of the com-
        bined operation against Vaagso, Norway, in December 1941.
        Had read Hutchinson's short story, "Excursion to Norway,"
        and had been struck by its evident factuality. Inquires the
        source of Hutchinson's information.

N.280. Raymond, Diana
        22 The Pryors, East Heath Road, London NW3. October 19,
        1964. "What is so wonderful, and so moving, is the way
        not only Stepan himself (in A Child Possessed), but the
        reader seems to come nearer to the child as the book goes
        on."

N.281. Frankau, Pamela
        55 Christchurch Hill, London NW3. "2nd." (?1964/1965).
        Describes A Child Possessed as "one of the most brilliant,
        beautiful and strong-boned novels I ever read ... if man got
        his desserts here below you'd be earning a Beatle's income."

N.282. Gittings, Robert
        44 Westgate, Chichester. January 13, 1965. "Just before
        Christmas I read A Child Possessed and was absolutely bowled
        over by it. It was not only that the re-creation of the place
        and a group of people was in your own special vein, and the

very best of that. It seemed to me that beyond the pictures that seemed to breathe, they were so real, there was a big philosophic idea that you had perfectly illustrated without ever letting the people who were acting it out become merely types or symbols. It remained always a drama, never just a morality. To me it was a kind of Greek tragedy, in modern dress."

N.283. Breckenridge, Caroline
Ravenswood Village Settlement for Mentally Handicapped Young People, Crowthorne, Berks. June 9 (?1965). Writer and her husband had bought a copy of A Child Possessed "with a view to our staff using it as a text-book, and to help them to understand the relationship between parents and handicapped children."

N.284. Hornby, Michael
Director, W.H. Smith & Son, Strand House, London WC2. July 21, 1966. Informs Hutchinson that he has won the W.H. Smith & Son Prize of £1,000 for A Child Possessed. "This award is made to a Commonwealth author whose book, originally written in English and published in the U.K., makes, in the opinion of the judges, the most outstanding contribution to literature during the period of the two years preceding the year of the award." (The judges were Rupert Hart-Davis, Margaret Lane and Raymond Mortimer.)

N.285. Raymond, Ernest
22 The Pryors, East Heath Road, London NW3. September 17, 1966. Informs Hutchinson that his latest novel, set in the Holy Land, has been dedicated to the novelist and his wife.

N.286. Feeny, Paddy
Yew Tree House, High Street, Ripley, Surrey. December 3, 1966. Thanks Hutchinson for allowing himself to be interviewed by the BBC about the W.H. Smith Prize, and congratulates him for being "one of the best interviewees that had been heard for a long time."

N.287. Taylor, John Russell
11 Hollytree Close, Inner Park Road, London SW19. February 17, 1968. Thanks Hutchinson for his kind letter about The Rise and Fall of the Well-Made Play.

N.288. Steiner, George
Churchill College, Cambridge. June 21, 1968. "I am most grateful for your letter. It is word from the novelist himself one needs & values most."

N.289. Severn, Derek

Strete Raleigh, Exlade Street, Woodcote, Reading. July 14, 1968. Thanks Hutchinson for his appreciation of the BBC talk on his work.

N.290. Raymond, Diana
22 The Pryors, East Heath Road, London NW3. April 14, 1969. Thanks Hutchinson for dedicating Johanna to her and to Ernest Raymond.

N.291. Church, Richard
The Priest's House, Sissinghurst Castle, Cranbrook, Kent. April 19, 1969. Church had just read Johanna at Daybreak and had been haunted by it, "another masterpiece." "As always in your novels, the conversion of idea and emotion into terms of something concrete, some action, atmosphere, event, place, is superb. This is the real art of fiction, the making as the poet makes." Johanna is "another novel to put alongside the immortals of the 19th century."

N.292. Raymond, Ernest
22 The Pryors, East Heath Road, London NW3. April 30, 1969. Hadn't then read Johanna, which had been dedicated to Diana and Ernest Raymond, but objects to Julian Symons' description of Hutchinson's style as "cliché-ridden."

N.293. Raymond, Diana
22 The Pryors, East Heath Road, London NW3. Undated (?April 1969). Had just read Johanna, and was deeply impressed, "haunting, beautiful, most terribly moving." She and Ernest Raymond very proud that it had been dedicated to them.

N.294. Day-Lewis, Sean
Daily Telegraph, Fleet Street, London EC4. Thursday November 10 (1969). Congratulates Hutchinson on A Child Possessed, "which we both lapped up and wept over," the prize and his speech.

N.295. Denham, Maurice and Margaret
29 Bedford Gardens, London W8. "Sunday" (November 13, 1969). Thanks Hutchinson for inviting them to the W.H. Smith presentation, "a splendid occasion," and congratulates him on his "marvellous" speech, "delivery and timing perfect."

N.296. Williams, Alan D.
Viking Press, 625 Madison Avenue, New York. February 22, 1971. Addressed to Hutchinson's US agent, John Cushman, 25 West 43rd St. Rejects Origins of Cathleen. "It needs cutting by a third in order to make certain those shining parts stand forth and unite in an effective whole."

N.297. Knopf, Alfred A. Inc.
201 East 50 St., New York. March 11, 1971. Addressed
to Cushman. Turns down Origins of Cathleen. Enjoyed the
comic parts but felt that the 'origins of Cathleen trick'
didn't work. "It's as if he decided that his basic material
wasn't sturdy enough to stand on its own, so invented a
gimmick to hold it together. The book should be left as a
wonderful childhood memoir, shorn of its portentousness
(the death of Kevin, etc.) and its romantic ending, and cut
severely."

N.298. Korda, Michael
Simon & Shuster, 630 Fifth Avenue, New York. March 17,
1971. Addressed to Cushman. Rejects Origins of Cathleen.
Enjoyed it but doesn't feel it would sell.

N.299. Putnam's, G.P. Sons
200 Madison Avenue, New York. August 5, 1971. Addressed
to Cushman. Rejects Origins of Cathleen: "the book mean-
ders without real direction until almost page 200."

N.300. Dodd, Mead
79 Madison Avenue, New York. December 28, 1971. Addressed to Cushman. Turns down Origins of Cathleen, "a
little slow-moving for American readers."

N.301. Scribner's, Charles Sons
597 Fifth Avenue, New York. March 1, 1972. Addressed to
Cushman. Rejects Origins of Cathleen as being too intricate
for the US market.

N.302. Fraser, Bruce
"Jonathan," St. Dogmael's, Cardigan. August 12, 1974.
Thanks Hutchinson for his appreciation of the revised ver-
sion of Gower's Complete Plain Words.

N.303. Severn, Derek
41 Langdale Place, Newtor Aycliffe, Co. Durham. December
16, 1974. Replying to Hutchinson's letter of August. "Sad-
dened by your despondence over your work." In that letter
Hutchinson had evidently described himself as a "passé author" and had also said that he had recently read the whole
of Proust.

N.304. Watson, Graham
Chairman, Curtis Brown Ltd., 1 Craven Hill, London W2
3EP. July 21, 1975. Addressed to Mrs. Margaret Hutchinson. Comments on Rising: "I am delighted to hear that
Ray's last novel was finished except for the ultimate chapter.
He always spoke to me about it as if it were in a way his
chef d'oeuvre, a testament of all that he believed in. I need

hardly say how much I am looking forward to reading it.
Of course if Jeremy (the novelist's son) feels that he can
complete it, so much the better. Judging from the obvious
sympathy that he had for his father and his writings, I
dare say he will do this with great skill and understanding.
Do please let me have it when it is in a state to be considered."

N.305. Watson, Graham
1 Craven Hill, London W2 3EP. September 29, 1975. Addressed to Mrs. Margaret Hutchinson. He has now read
Rising, with Jeremy Hutchinson's conclusion, and will send
it off to Michael Joseph. Comments: "My own feeling is
that the book should stop at the point where Ray left it but
carrying your own comment in much its present form. I
think your son has made a good shot at the extra pages but
they seem to me flat and adding nothing to a book where
the main theme has been stated and what is absent can be
left to the reader's imagination. If you read again the meeting between father and daughter I think perhaps you would
agree that it is totally anticlimatic [sic] to the dazzling material which proceeds [sic] it."

N.306. Watson, Graham
1 Craven Hill, London W2 3EP. October 8, 1975. Reports
that Anthea Joseph wants to publish Rising though the royalties must be modest because of its length. Watson recommends acceptance of £1000 advance against 10 percent to
4,000 copies, 12 1/2 percent to 6,000, 15 percent thereafter.
Joseph is willing to accept Jeremy Hutchinson's conclusion,
but Watson again recommends it be excluded. Reports that
he has sent off the other typescript to America.

N.307. Farrar, Margaret (Mrs. John Farrar)
16 East 96th Street, New York. December 3, 1975. Addressed to Mrs. Margaret Hutchinson. Has arranged with
Roger Straus that she shall read the typescript of Rising.

N.308. Watson, Graham
1 Craven Hill, London W2 3EP. February 16, 1976. Addressed to Mrs. Margaret Hutchinson. Reports that Harper's, New York, has rejected Rising.

N.309. Farrar, Margaret
March 26, 1976. Addressed to Mrs. Margaret Hutchinson.
Reports that she has at last got the typescript of Rising
from Roger Straus and has begun reading it, with great enjoyment.

N.310. Farrar, Margaret
April 1, 1976. Addressed to Mrs. Margaret Hutchinson. Re-

ports that she has finished <u>Rising</u> and returned it to Straus who will forward it to their second reader, Robert Giroux, the friend and editor of T.S. Eliot.

N.311. Farrar, Margaret
April 11, 1976. Addressed to Mrs. Margaret Hutchinson. Offers her condolences on the refusal by Farrar, Straus & Giroux of <u>Rising</u>, on the grounds of length and cost. Reveals that the typescript she saw was confused at the ending, and didn't have the "Postscript."

N.312. Scott, Paul
78 Addison Way, London NW11 6QS. July 30, 1976. "Dear Mrs Hutchinson/ I am sending this note through M(ichael). J(oseph). The review copy of "Rising" has just reached me. I haven't begun to read it because its pubn date, Sep 6, is beyond my current copy & dead-line date but I hope very much to have read it in order to write something about it for the subsequent issue (Sep 9), which will actually be my last review in CL (<u>Country Life</u>) for some time because I'm then spending the Autumn Term at an American University (heaven help me!)/ The reason I write to you is to say that quite apart from my admiration of R.C. Hutchinson as a writer I remember him as an officer in the 8 Buffs,--B, Company, I think, (Dropmore & Devon, July 1940 on). I was a newly joined recruit in D Company, but I had friends in Capt Hutchinson's Co, & I can tell you that these young men (in B. Co), as we all were in those days, young, I mean, thought themselves lucky to have <u>him</u> for a Company Commander, & not the others, & that the one or two of these friends who were transferred to D Company from B (have I really got the names right?: I think so) deeply regretted it./ The reason was of course that Capt Hutchinson was a good man. I saw him quite often (but never spoke to him) & was much impressed to be looking at & in the presence of a man who had already done what I hoped one day to do myself--write novels. Years & years later he was good enough to come to a talk I was giving & I told him the circumstances in which we had 'met' before. We had a good laugh. But the thing is, he was much <u>honoured</u> by the young soldiers he had charge of. I thought you might like to know, because I gather he thought his military career rather unsuccessful--but it wasn't, so far as young recruits were concerned--& that was important, & I wanted to say it to you./ All this has nothing to do with R.C. Hutchinson as a writer, of course. I hope it doesn't bore you to hear it. But he was the man in that Battalion I never heard a bad word against, & I wish he had been in command of me. I didn't tell him that, when we met officially at the RSL (Royal Society of Literature), but it's what I feel, & because <u>Country Life</u> have enclosed

a letter from M(ichael). Joseph suggesting that you think I
might like to see "Rising" I thought I'd drop you a line,
just to record this indelible memory of him--with his stick,
his mittens (winter), a moustache (surely), & a smile & a
look in the eye that reminded us we were all still human
beings--/Sincerely/Paul Scott."

(Scott died before he could review Rising for Country Life.)

N.313.   Raymond, Diana
         22 The Pryors, East Heath Road, London NW3 1BS. August
         23, 1976. Addressed to Mrs. Margaret Hutchinson. Recalls
         that it was the arrival of her and "Betty" that made Hutchin-
         son put down his pen for the last time. Praises Rising as
         a "magnificent" novel.

N.314.   Horder, Mervyn
         4 Hamilton Close, London NW8 8QY. September 15 (1976).
         Addressed to Mrs Margaret Hutchinson. Informs her that
         he has reviewed Rising for PEN Bulletin. "I had the feeling
         that he had reached a sort of ecstasy in finding the story
         panning out so exactly in accordance with his own high
         ideals--and that for an artist that is not a bad moment to
         die." Attaches list of 15 literals in the text.

N.315.   Joseph, Anthea
         Michael Joseph Ltd., 52 Bedford Square, London WC1B 3EF.
         September 20, 1976. Addressed to Mrs. Margaret Hutchin-
         son. Acknowledges (?Horder's) corrections that she had
         received from Mrs. Hutchinson and comments on the slip
         over "C Day Lewis." (On jacket, his name appeared as
         C.S. Lewis.)

N.316.   Skinner, Martyn
         Ilex House, Fitzhead, Taunton. November 8, 1976. Ad-
         dressed to Mrs. Margaret O. Hutchinson. Praises Hutchin-
         son's marvellous recreation of place in Rising, "far more
         vividly and impressively than Conrad in Nostromo." Re-
         marks on his ability, like Austen in Emma, to make even
         dull characters interesting. Wonders if there might possibly
         have been too many journeys in the novel and too much
         straight description of landscape. Praises Hutchinson's por-
         trayal of Sabino's change ("metanoia") and the triumphant
         invention of the German monastery.

N.317.   Gittings, Robert & Jo
         The Stables, East Dean, Chichester. November 23, 1976.
         Addressed to Mrs. Margaret Hutchinson. Praises Rising
         for its blending of physical and spiritual experience. Com-
         pares it with the "spiritual allegories of W.H. Hudson, like
         Green Mansions."

O. Schoolboy Diary

O.318. R.C. Hutchinson kept a diary between January 1, 1923 and
July 22, 1923 while he was at school at Monkton Combe,
Bath, the entries ending on the last day of the summer
term. (This diary is deposited in MOHC.) The following
are excerpts from that diary:

January 1, 1923
"Have decided to write a diary of thought, since my life
consists, I think, more in thought than in deed." On New
Year's Day, 1923, he walked from Ludgate Hill to Bond
Street "in order to see life." (This was the Christmas holiday, which Hutchinson would have spent with his parents in
London.) He was deeply upset by the sight of "a little old
man, who was lame, and haggard," and who was the only
person who did not say "happy new year." Records that
he does not believe in the chance of happiness.

January 6, 1923
"I think one day, if ever I am so energetic, I shall write a
novel on the parent problem. How love remains, but opin-
ions get so widely different." (A reference to the difficulties Hutchinson faced in the relationship with his evangelical father.)

January 14, 1923
"There is another thing I want to do. That is to write a
novel or drama illustrating this wild chase after happiness
which constitutes an important part of our existence. Of
course Hardy has already done something of the sort."

January 24, 1923
"But I will make money, somehow. Possibly I could write; I
feel that I have materials for a best-seller, but my style
would never go down."

February 8, 1923
"The spirit of French Rev. was socialism, and socialism is
or should be the great ideal."

February 27, 1923
"I am getting more and more convinced about socialism.
You know we must give everyone a chance. They are not
like ourselves, but they are made in our likeness."

February 28, 1923
"I have put a poem in "The Monktonian" which will rather
settle scores with young Jeremy, on the Corps business."

March 8, 1923
Records a visit to Bath(?) Abbey with an aunt. "What interests me most are the little stones, tucked away behind the big ones; very few people seem to notice them. 'Here lies Mary Smith. Born 1716. Died 1773.' What was Mary Smith like, I wonder. Possibly the Abbey charters would have something about her."

April 5, 1923
"In town today. (For the Easter holiday.) Gorgeous Blackfriars. Yes, the class system must go; it is mucking everything. Each hols tell me the same thing."

June 10, 1923
"Have started 'Poor Relations.' (Balzac) Seems damned good; but inhuman in some respects."

June 17, 1923
"Yes, Poor Relations was good, very good. Excellent technique, clear (but I cannot think brilliant) style, and good humour. Characters very well done, and motive well worked out. I really enjoyed every page of it, so much so that I finished it in the week; which is a testimony of slackness. Impetigo not much better."

July 1, 1923
"I want to fill this book as much as possible with the various ideas that come into my head. Then I will have something to draw on for novels, etc--if I ever write any."

P. Notebooks

Several of Hutchinson's notebooks, containing ideas for his novels, are deposited in MOHC. The following are some of the more interesting entries:

P.319. General Comment About Fiction
"The novel may have a philosophical theme, but not a political theme--the difference being that a political theme binds the characters to certain courses of action and puts them into certain moral uniforms--e.g. a leftist novel will force its writer to make all his rich characters either to some extent cruel or to some extent stupid." (Undated notebook entry.)

P.320. ELEPHANT AND CASTLE
"Girl who 'reclaims' criminal and marries him. Criminal does not respond. Gradually revealed that criminal has the real

virtues, honesty, etc, while girl is really moral poseuse."
(Undated entry from "Plots Book," perhaps 1940 when the
novel was "designed.")

P.321.   RECOLLECTION OF A JOURNEY
Entry (?late 1948) recording the table of events in the novel.

1847	Stanislas born
1863	S (at 16) takes part in the insurrection. Betrayed by peasant (?). Sentenced to 10 years in Siberia.
1873	S returns from Siberia.
1884	S marries Jadwiga (b. 1868).
1885	Julius born.
1886	Alexandra born.
1904	Julius marries Alexandra.
1905	Victor born. Augustus takes part in rising. Betrayed. Sentenced 2 years in Kadorka.
1906	Stefanie born and Casimir born.
1910	Peasant's cottage burned under observation of Henryk. Rescue of Stefanie by Alexandra.
1914	Stefanie sent to Zurich.
1917	Birth of Wanda.
1923	First marriage of Stefanie (to Casimir).
1924	Birth of Annetta. Desertion of Stefanie's husband.
1925	Stefanie (19) returns to Poland, to become governess to Wanda (8).
1932	Return of Victor from foreign service (?).
1933	Marrying of Stefanie and Victor.
1934	First miscarrying.
1936	Second miscarrying.
1939	Novel opens (Sept.).

P.322.   RECOLLECTION OF A JOURNEY
A note, undated, on the style required for the novel.
"The style must have the quality of limpidity. It must have
a music. It must be flexible, so as to carry factual matter
and descriptions of sordid realities as well as subtle descriptions of psychical states. But above all it must, in itself,
represent the hallucinatory feeling of the story. It must also
be feminine."

P.323.   RECOLLECTION OF A JOURNEY
Undated synopsis.
"Stefanie was born of peasant stock. When she was four
years old the cottage in which her parents lived was burnt
in revenge by the Chubarovs, her parents shot down. She
was rescued and taken care of by a sister of Julius, and
brought up in the Chubarovs' home up to the age of 8. She
is then sent to a convent school in Switzerland. In 1920
she moves to the university of Geneva, where Casimir Chu-
barov is also studying. They fall in love and marry. An-

netta is born. Casimir, falling in love with a girl he pities,
deserts her. She returns to the home of the Chubarovs,
who keep her in return for her service as a governess to
their child Wanda. 1932 Casimir dies. Victor takes her off
and marries her. They live in city (and service stations).
Miscarriages in 1934 and 1936.

"1939 (Sept). Victor away with the army. Their house destroyed. Tells her to go to Chubarovs--Julius will meet
her at the station. She, Annetta and Victor travel together--
see Julius' house burn.

"At Chubarovs' house she waits for her child, the coming of
the Russians. Goes over the past. Learns more of her origins (?) begins to suspect the Chubarovs. Visit of Victor--
unsatisfactory.

"All taken to Siberia. Development under stress of their
characters. Her plot for vengeance upon Julius and Jadwiga.
Birth and death of her son. Birth of a son to Annetta (A
will not say whose it is, and S suspects Henryk). Liaison
between S and Henryk or Julius. Return of Victor, muti-
lated.

"The evacuation across the Caspian."

P.324.   IMAGE OF MY FATHER
Undated note.
"David Selborne, eccentric, recluse, died in October 1943."

P.325.   ORIGINS OF CATHLEEN
Notebook entry dated April 26, 1962.
"? Next novel. English family. Fairly comic but profound.
Autobiographical--perhaps written as if it were my own auto-
biography. Amused but affectionate."

P.326.   ORIGINS OF CATHLEEN
Hutchinson's draft of a response to a questionnaire from
Michael Joseph Ltd. (?in 1971).
"Perhaps every writer lives in fear of getting into a rut--
of delivering, in ideas or in style, the mixture as before.
When I finished Johanna at Daybreak, a sombre story, I felt
the need to write in an entirely different mood. There is in
Origins of Cathleen a serious theme, centred on a young
Irishman whose general behaviour conceals a deep perplexity;
but the story is presented mainly as comedy. I discovered
the comedy I needed by exploring, with elderly eyes, a
small boy of ludicrous fancies and appalling self-esteem: it
was helpful to find myself strangely, disquietingly familiar
with the mental processes of that insufferable child. He has
portrayed himself with only a little professional guidance
from me."

P.327.   RISING
         Hutchinson's draft of a response to a questionnaire from
         Michael Joseph Ltd. (? in 1971).
         "I am in the planning stage of a novel, with a theme that
         seems to me important, which has been germinating for some
         time past; a book which will probably take me two or three
         years to write."

P.328.   RISING
         Hutchinson's notes for the 'blurb' for the novel.
         "Ostensibly the study of an episode in South American his-
         tory, is at a deeper level an examination of racial and other
         human relationships, of the tragedy of alienation ... the
         eternal problem of evil. It hints a key/solution/answer to
         that problem.

         "The writing is vivid, exact, sometimes ironic, sometimes
         eloquent. In the description of a desperate march it achieves
         something in the nature of poetry.

         "The contrasting characters of Sabino and his son Patricio...

         "Those readers who consider R.C. Hutchinson's writing to
         be a positive contribution...

         "Amalgam of realism and poetic interpretation.

         "Safe to say that it differs in theme and scope from most of
         today's recent fiction."

P.329.   RISING
         A foolscap sheet entitled "Questions," relating to the end of
         the novel.
         "1. The state of things at El Cubo. Has El Cubo too been
              wrecked? Presumably the main characters there are
              still alive and in reasonable order anyway!
         "2. What about the servants, farmhands, at Quinta El
              Duque? Are any left? Where have the rest got to?
              Are they likely to return?
         "3. Has Diego known hitherto about the death of Benicia?
         "4. Where exactly is Diego to meet Sabino, e.g. in dining
              room? in D's own house? In other words, how is next
              bit to open? Mem: that S and Y are both desperately
              in need of sleep.
         "5. Is S. to encounter the Papac cousin (Atun Papac)--or
              other guerillero(s) at e.g. El Cubo?
         "6. Who is to straighten out S's thoughts/emotions--Diego
              or Marta? And when?
         "7. Can the one conversation--Diego/Sabino--cover both in-
              formation & spiritual guidance?
         "8. Is it feasible that Diego should go with him to El Cubo?

(Perhaps better that he goes quite alone, leaving Y to
help Diego. 'I promise to send you Deseada.')"

P.330. RISING
The notebook for the novel contains material under the fol-
lowing heads: Principles, Questions, Schema, Possible
Names, Vocabulary, Animal Life, Vegetation, People, Odd
Details, Food & Drink, Diseases, Diagram (of the geography).
Under "Principles" Hutchinson noted:
"7.   Poetry. Nervous style, enriched by observation of the
      curious & beautiful. Beware of over-elaborate sen-
      tences, paragraphs.
"8.   Family Relationships. Somewhat Proustian. A certain
      lack of intimacy, perhaps, but a tired, defensive sense
      of holding together in a common cause--surviving (with-
      out effort), preserving their industrial empire--which
      the influence of y [Atun Papac] threatens."

"It is of the first importance to delineate carefully the idea
of violent revolution against that of revolution-by-love. The
violent revolutionary's ideas--impatience, despair, practical-
ity, etc: etc:--must be carefully and sympathetically studied."

"November 9, 1970. Towards the end x's [Sabino's] wife
might be dying and a sort of reconciliation might take place.
He might try to get her to y [Papac] for healing--she would
die on the way."

"There are 3 forces in operation.
(i)   x [Sabino]--representing power/staus/wealth (roughly)
(ii)   the form of revolutionary protest, headed by an intel-
       ligent, resolute, ruthless man.
(iii) the ultimately winning force of love represented by
       y [Papac]. (iii) needs to be hinted at--planted deli-
       cately--all the way through the book. It is the one
       which x cannot cope with because of his spiritual
       poverty, of which he is always vaguely aware--and
       for which he compensates himself by violence."

The Schema includes the following note for Part IV
"Fresh development (Summer '71). Having returned home,
and found Quinta el Duce sacked and his wife very ill, he
sets out to take her to Papac. She dies on the way--recon-
ciliation--but he goes on with the body (and with his ser-
vant) towards La T."

In the section entitled "Vocabulary" there is a reference to
the index and glossary of Fawcett's book, and most of Hutchinson's notes on this subject seem to be drawn from Fawcett. He also read Prescott's History of the Conquest of
Mexico (1843) and Blakemore's Latin America, especially the

notes at the beginning and the important memoranda at the end.

In another notebook, in which he jotted down details of places he visited in South America, he wrote:
"One wants to show finally Reo Papac's influence overcoming the revolutionaries as well as Sabino; to suggest that one solution is always waiting, to be applied to every problem of conduct, political, social, etc."

In this same notebook Hutchinson made a note to read Che Guevara and Mao Tse-Tung's, Guerilla Warfare (Cassell, 1962) and Guevara's Bolivian Diary (Cape, 1968).

Hutchinson also noted down the chronology of the novel in a notebook:

> Story opens in 1904.
> Sabino born 1855, adopted 1861.
> Destruction Cubiquite 1884
> Sabino married in 1877
>   met Iloa in 1878
> Sabino's mother born 1825
> Father born 1820, died in 1904.

However, elsewhere in his notes he places the setting of the novel in 1903.

Q. Account Book

Q.331. Hutchinson kept a detailed record of all his literary earnings from 1928 to 1964 in an account book, deposited in MOHC. This fascinating record enables us to chart with great precision the rise and fall in his commercial reputation, as in the graph on p. 73 and below. His first earnings as a writer in fact date back as early as 1917, when, at the age of nine, he received two guineas from Lady Haig as the prize for an essay on "War Models." The figures in the columns below record his total earnings, year by year, and details of the larger items:

1928	Ŀ9.2.0.	Ŀ7 for "Every Twenty Years."
1929	Ŀ25.11.1	Ŀ11 for "To Commerce via the University."
1930	Ŀ55.17.8	Ŀ26.16.8 for Thou Hast A Devil.
1931	Ŀ14.14.0	
1932	Ŀ240.1.5	Ŀ89.19.3 for Answering Glory and Ŀ116.3.4 as US advance on Answering Glory.

1933	Ł95.2.4.	Ł88.14.7 (Ł100 gross) English advance for Unforgotten Prisoner.
1934	Ł879.16.0	Ł606.12.0 English royalties on Unforgotten Prisoner.
1935	Ł709.9.10	Ł453.15.6. English advance for One Light Burning.
1936	Ł531.19.0	Ł450 advance on Shining Scabbard.
1937	Ł1763.7.6.	Ł712 from Bookclub for Shining Scabbard; Ł666 US royalties, mostly on the latter.
1938	Ł994.5.11.	Ł450 advance on Testament and Ł310 for US advance on Shining Scabbard.
1939	Ł1384.19.1	Ł914 Testament royalties.
1940	Ł1851	Ł450 advance on The Fire and the Wood; Ł987 for US serial rights to the latter.
1941	Ł1615.9.0	Ł1534 for US royalties.
1942	Ł341.2.3.	Old royalties only.
1943	Ł167.3.0.	Old royalties only.
1944	Ł559.14.7.	Ł450 (Ł500 gross) for Interim.
1945	Ł1258.13.4.	Ł285 US advance on Interim; Ł417 English royalties on The Fire and the Wood and Interim.
1946	Ł747.0.5	Ł133 Danish royalties on Testament.
1947	Ł868.8.9.	
1948	Ł412.0.11	Ł225 first half of advance on Elephant and Castle.
1949	Ł3574.12.7.	Ł2163 from America for Elephant; Ł467 second half of English advance; Ł1105 English royalties for Elephant.
1950	Ł3267.18.3	Ł2560 from Rinehart for Elephant.
1951	Ł2746.15.0	Ł2560 from Rinehart.
1952	Ł3450.18.5.	Ł2560 from Rinehart; Ł811 from Cassell's for Recollection of a Journey.
1953	Ł3007.16.0	Ł2540 from US.
1954	Ł814.9.7.	Ł357 from US; Ł225 first advance on The Stepmother.
1955	Ł1036.0.1.	Remainder of British advance on latter; Ł321 US advance on The Stepmother.
1956	Ł1806.1.7.	Ł1039 from Rinehart; Ł321 as option on dramatic rights to The Stepmother in US.
1957	Ł2107.1.1.	Ł450 British advance on March The Ninth; Ł641 US advance on the same novel; Ł640 Twentieth Century-Fox film option.
1958	Ł2028.7.0.	Ł1116 Bles royalties.
1959	Ł3981.19.4.	Hutchinson's most fruitful year: Ł1557 from Bookclub for March The Ninth; Ł1828 from film sale of The Stepmother.

1960	Ŀ467.2.7.	Ŀ244 Bles royalties on March The Ninth.
1961	Ŀ1940.11.10	Ŀ450 Bles advance on Image of My Father; Ŀ963 US advance on the same novel.
1962	Ŀ314.6.0	
1963	Ŀ675.2.11	Ŀ600 advance from Curtis Brown, agents.
1964	Ŀ1653.17.9	Ŀ450 Bles advance on A Child Possessed; Ŀ963 US advance on the same novel.

SUMMARY Hutchinson's total literary income for the 37 recorded years was thus some Ŀ47,397, an average yearly income of about Ŀ1,281. (He did not start writing full time until 1935, and lost five years to military service between 1940 and 1945.)

GRAPH SHOWING HUTCHINSON'S LITERARY INCOME: 1931-1964

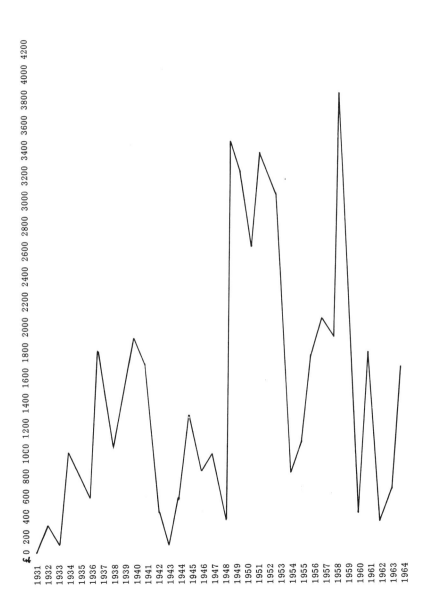

SECTION THREE: SECONDARY MATERIAL

R. General Studies of Hutchinson's Work

R.332. Anon., Wilson Library Bulletin (May 1939).

R.333. Anon., Obituary, The Times (July 5, 1975), 14.

R.334. Bagnall, Stephen, "R.C. Hutchinson: The Man and the Novelist." Paper delivered to Manchester Literary Society,
October 1957.

R.335. Bentley, Phyllis, "Is the British Novel Dead?" Saturday Review of Literature, XIX (January 28, 1939), 3-4, 14.

R.336. Church, Richard, "Introduction," Shining Scabbard (Duckworth, London: 1968).

R.337. Cormack, M. Grant, "R.C. Hutchinson," Focus (January
1959), 16-18.

R.338. _____, "Characters with High Ideals," Christian Advo-
cate (April 25, 1959), 3.

R.339. Cox, Kenneth, "The Novels of R.C. Hutchinson," Scripsi
(Melbourne), II, ii/iii (Spring 1983), 117-124.

R.340. Cunningham, Valentine, "Hauntings and Holocaust," The
Times Literary Supplement, 4199 (September 23, 1983), 1010.

R.341. Delaney, Frank, "R.C. Hutchinson Reappraised." Talk
broadcast on BBC Radio Four, February 1, 1981.

R.342. Endersby, Elisabeth, Unpublished thesis on Johanna at Daybreak, submitted to Rachel McMillan College of Education,
March 1977.

R.343. Flint, F.C., "Recent Fiction," Southern Review, II (Spring
1937), 835-855.

R.344. Foster, William, Interview with R.C. Hutchinson, Scotsman
(March 7, 1970).

R.345. Gilman, Ian, Discussion of Testament with Gilbert Phelps in
"Good Books," broadcast on BBC World Service, March 12,
1982.

R.346. Gillett, Eric ("Aquilla"), "Best Male Novelist?" The Leader
(February 17, 1945), 16.

R.347. Green, Robert, "The Novels of R.C. Hutchinson," English
Studies in Africa, XXVI, i (March 1983), 39-56.

R.348. _____, "Paiforce: The Novelist as Military Historian,"
Army Quarterly and Defence Journal (April 1985).

R.349. _____, "Afterword," The Quixotes: Collected Stories of

R.C. Hutchinson (Carcanet Press, Manchester: 1984), pp. 227-8.

R.350. Hart-Davis, Sir Rupert, Obituary, The Times (July 9, 1975), 16.

R.351. _____, "Introduction," Two Men of Letters (Michael Joseph, London: 1979), pp. 9-18.

R.352. Horder, Mervyn, "One Light Burning: The World of R.C. Hutchinson," London Magazine, XVII (December 1977), 65-72.

R.353. Jones, Allan, "The Novels of R.C. Hutchinson," Proteus, IV (November 1978), 7-13.

R.354. Lloyd, Canon Roger, "Layman's Ministry of Print, IV--R.C. Hutchinson," Church Times (December 28, 1951).

R.355. Phelps, Gilbert, "Contemporary Writers, No. IV: R.C. Hutchinson." Talk broadcast on BBC External Service, August 1967.

R.356. Pick, J.B., Essay on Hutchinson in Reginald Moore, ed., Modern Reading XV (Phoenix, London: 1947).

R.357. Prebble, K.R., Critical Introduction to Hutchinson's work in James Vinson, ed., Contemporary Novelists (St. James Press, London: 1972), pp. 658-659.

R.358. Severn, Derek, "R.C. Hutchinson: A Neglected Genius." Talk broadcast on BBC Radio Three, September 4, 1976. Reprinted as "The Hutchinson Question," The Listener (September 9, 1976), 318.

R.359. _____, Untitled essay on R.C. Hutchinson, New Fiction, IX (October 1976), 21.

S. Reviews of Hutchinson's Novels

THOU HAST A DEVIL

S.360. Nottingham Guardian (October 20, 1930).
Some clever characterization and much humor. Remarkably fine first novel. "The narrative is consistent all through the book, the pace is fast and constant, the humour abundant, the observation of character shrewd, and the mystical undercurrent remains an unobtrusive, yet influential, undercurrent." (Hutchinson's first review.)

S.361. Morning Post (October 24, 1930).
"There is more promise than actual achievement in this unusual novel." Characterization is dominated by the needs of the fable, "but Mr Hutchinson has ideas and imagination and should do good work in the future."

S.362. Nottingham Journal (October 31, 1930).
Courageous attempt at a difficult task makes novel worthy of

wide attention. Vision of future is convincing: "certainties,
such as television and private aeroplanes, a possibility, such
as a regular airship service to the Far East, and wilder
flights of fancy [sic], such as self-rule for negroes [sic],
all fit neatly into place without impeding the course of the
story." Praises the naturalness of the conversation and the
novel's wit, but criticizes it for having too much "unneces-
sary explanation," and for the vagueness of Diana. Praises
Khamhaïv who is portrayed "with just the right amount of
sympathy and sincerity." Notes the novel's "intensity of
purpose." "Its original theme and genuine, sturdy thoughts
make it an outstanding publication."

S.363. The Times Literary Supplement (November 13, 1930).
"Mr Hutchinson possesses such a vivid imagination that he
has elected to write of a visionary land during the years to
come." Reviewer then summarizes the novel's plot.

THE ANSWERING GLORY

S.364. V.S. Pritchett, New Statesman (April 2, 1932).
Novel "collapses into shapeless triviality after a few pages,"
though the missionary and the trader are "characters with
possibilities."

S.365. The Times Literary Supplement (April 14, 1932).
Miss Thompson "a memorable character."

S.366. Norman Collins, Daily News (April 20, 1932).
Hutchinson "not yet a complete novelist. But he can communicate the fascination of strange places and can suggest
the heroism of lonely duty."

S.367. The Guardian (May 20, 1932).
Notes that the title comes from a Stevenson poem, and praises
the ending as "vague yet eminently apposite."

S.368. New York Times Book Review (June 5, 1932).
"The force and subtlety of this book lies in its simplicity."
Notes that the Maharo scenes "are in a minor key, unde-
tailed and unemphatic, forming merely the unchanging background against which her character, her real self, makes
the essential pattern." Novel "contains little incident but
much really skillful analysis and development of character;
and perhaps we may be forgiven for saying that the pictures
of girls' school life hit the mark almost too incredibly accurately to come from the pen of a man." (First major US review.)

S.369. Margaret Cheney Dawson, New York Herald Tribune (June 5,
1932).

"It is, despite its gentleness, an uncompromising tale, one which stands squarely on the ground that godliness and courage are fine themes for any book, and which does not wander down other paths for so much as a single sentence. It has no kinship with the 'exposés' in which the breakdown of Christian morale in the tropics is used for bait, nor does the author exploit the natives for literary effect." "Although there are times when the sheer goodness of Miss Thompson and her co-workers seems almost oppressive, the attitude of author and characters throughout is distinct from sentimentality. It is simply a frank acknowledgement of reverence for beliefs which have of late been questioned and attacked on all sides."

THE UNFORGOTTEN PRISONER

S.370. Hugh Walpole, John O'London's Weekly (December 2, 1933). Best novel of 1933 by a new author. Novel is very bold. Hutchinson "dares melodrama, sentiment, anything that he feels necessary. And brilliantly he succeeds."

S.371. Arthur Waugh, Spectator (December 8, 1933). Places Hutchinson in the realistic tradition of Gissing and George Moore. "His atmosphere and his effects depend upon a laborious accumulation of minutiae; he sees everything in high relief; and lingers as tenderly as Holman Hunt over the painting of a shaving or a jewel." Badly constructed, though, and reviewer objects to the combination of first- and third-person narrative, and to the rapid switches of scene. Theme of novel is the temperamental antagonism of Germany and England.

S.372. Lionel Hale, News Chronicle (December 13, 1933). "A very fine novel indeed. It is also extremely ill-planned; it is marred by mistimed levity; it begins by being founded on improbability, it goes on by being much too long and it ends by being obscure. I haven't enjoyed a novel so much for months." Hutchinson "has so many arrows, he disdains a shield." "Mr Hutchinson has a mind, and its vigour and clarity are stamped on every sentence he writes; he has an eye and doesn't bother if there are motes in it. What a novel! Full of holes as a sieve, it holds water."

S.373. James Agate, Daily Express (December 14, 1933). "Portrays the England of Galsworthy without Galsworthy's talent." Novel is "snobbish" and pretentious.

S.374. The Times Literary Supplement (December 14, 1933). Uneven in quality with virtues "of the solid and slightly old-fashioned kind." "The sentiment towards the end is a little

overdone and, like the humorous embellishments, blurs the
outline of a very credible piece of invention."

S.375. Peter Quennell, New Statesman (December 16, 1933).
Obvious faults (badly constructed and too long), but "the
story leaves behind it an impression sharper and more
permanent than that of the average modern novel." Hutchinson seems to write well "largely by literary instinct" and
"is incapable of distinguishing between the good and bad
elements in his work." "The characteristics of his style at
its most impressive are solidity, clarity and a certain effect
of gloomy, rather nightmarish, concentration." John Sag-
gard a "painfully facetious" narrator, though Hutchinson
writes simply, vividly and energetically about Klaus.

S.376. Edwin Muir, The Listener (December 20, 1933).
A commonplace, complacent novel. "The author says many
true things, but they are somewhat commonplace; he expresses a humane and enlightened attitude, but it is somewhat complacent." The inadequacy of Hutchinson's de-
cency and humanity, though the novel is "respectable, intelligent, serious, edifying." When Hutchinson escapes
from his "professional seriousness" he can write with genuine power, as in Klaus' escape from the Abbey. Surmises
that novelist understands boys, but not adults: "his adults,
indeed, are boys in disguise."

S.377. Compton Mackenzie, Daily Mail (December 21, 1933).
"The best English novel that has been published this year,
and one of the half-dozen best English novels written since
the War." The symphonic effect of the novel's construction:
"The kind of novel that I feel Beethoven would have appreciated."

S.378. T.S. Matthews, New Republic (February 28, 1934).
"Though the book is marred by that deep-seated, sly sentimentality of which only Englishmen are capable, and which
takes the twin forms of introducing malapropos humor and
cutting out all direct expressions of sentiment, its effect as
a whole is noble."

ONE LIGHT BURNING

S.379. Bonamy Dobrée, Morning Post (February 12, 1935).
Novel "written ... not only with humour, but with terrific
narrative drive and profound understanding, added to what
appears to be an intimate knowledge of out of the way places
and people. It is seldom that one meets a novel which gives
one such a complete illusion of the reality of the characters
and the things they were engaged in, and is so triumphantly
yet unsentimentally poignant."

S.380. The Scotsman (February 14, 1935).
"Mr Hutchinson is not an easy writer, although his actual
manner of expressing himself is lucid and attractive. It is
rather the fullness of incident, the diversity of action and
character which he manages to condense into comparatively
few words that necessitate his work being read slowly and
with close attention." Hutchinson an author who impresses
by the force of his personality.

S.381. The Times (February 15, 1935).
In the novel a "heroic adventure is combined with all the
elements of a drama of character." His geography will pose
problems to some readers. Magnificent account of the journey. The ending "managed very dexterously and persua-
sively."

S.382. Cyril Connolly, New Statesman (February 16, 1935).
"An earnest, mystificating novel. A typical middlebrow
book, full of chaste, philosophical, quixotic Englishmen."

S.383. Rayner Heppenstall, Yorkshire Post (February 20, 1935).
"Largeness of conception and ... fullness of reality." "Definitely, Mr Hutchinson is competing with the giants of literature."

S.384. The Times Literary Supplement (February 21, 1935).
The "old heroic values" of the novel, "a long and carefully
constructed story, packed with excitement and credible
enough from start to finish." Criticizes the uncertainty of
the geography but one "is carried along by the thrill of the
chase and by the alternating currents of stern and romantic
humanity." Splendid description of Andrew's journey. "An
invigorating and attractive piece of work."

S.385. Compton Mackenzie, Daily Mail (February 21, 1935).
Hutchinson is "the best male novelist his generation has
produced in England ... a genuine creative artist. Mr
Hutchinson is essentially a romantic, and nowadays a man
must be endowed with the courage that only a consciousness
of his own originality can give, if he is to be a successful
romantic." Hutchinson's ability to persuade readers of the
reality of his created world against the dictates of their
own common sense. Novel "is a tale of noble adventure. It
is a tale of a great love. It is a tale of self-sacrifice. It
carries the reader, with the conviction that he is under-
going an actual experience, from a seaport in Wales up the
Baltic ports to reach Siberia. It offers a gallery of strange
but always credible portraits. Above all it extends the imagination and demolishes a great deal of contemporary futility."

S.386. Isabel Paterson, New York Herald Tribune (February 24,
1935).

Describes novel as a "romance." "The substance of romance
is always a conflict between the human soul and its material
circumstances. A conviction of the profound importance of
the human being as such, not as a material or physical cog
in some cosmic machinery but as being possessed of free will
and value in his own right, must be expressed in action.
Mr Hutchinson writes from that premise." Makes the point
that Wild "avoided women, because he liked them ... a bachelor
by conviction, not by temperament." Criticizes Hutchinson's
geography: "place names and routes are deplorably confusing." Similarly, the obscure names. But "one gets the
feel of the cold, the desolation of a sub-Arctic landscape."
Also praises the characterization of the idealist Andrew and
the Bolshevik bureaucrats.

S.387. William Plomer, Spectator (March 1, 1935).
Finds novel "unsatisfying." "There can be no question of
the seriousness of Mr Hutchinson's intentions, but they are
carried out with such a mixture of the abrupt and the dif-
fuse that it is as difficult to keep one's bearings as it is to
feel that he has found on this occasion a suitable vehicle for
his descriptive and other gifts."

S.388. Laura Benet, New York Evening Sun (March 1, 1935).
"In spite of the rough-and-tumble virility of the narration
with its continual grasp of the actual, this is the record
of a spiritual experience." Badly constructed--too much
space at the beginning to the Brissauts--and reviewer finds
the last chapter, Grundmann's return, "totally unconvincing."
Yet the characters and places are overwhelmingly vivid. "In
this day and time it is startling to find a novelist of ability
whose hero is pure idealist, whose theme is vaguely spiritual,
whose country of the soul reveals a blankness like that of
the Siberian steppes--yet who finally leaves readers with a
sensation of hope in eternal things."

S.389. Arthur Ruhl, Saturday Review of Literature (March 2, 1935).
"He has power and what in actors is called 'authority,' spiritual earnestness, and can, when he chooses, spring sur-
prises and create suspense. At the same time, his trick of
deliberate obscurity, of knowingness about all sorts of things
which the reader is unable to share, can become irritating,
and in the matter of being solemn to the point of absurdity,
he sails pretty close to the wind." Notes that the title comes
from a Sassoon poem. "This more or less mystical pursuit
of the ideal grinds desperately on throughout the novel
against a background always vivid, realistic up to a certain
point--the point of permitting the reader to understand just
what country or neighbourhood he actually is in--curiously
spattered with exotic details, unfamiliar coins, drinks, and
what not, and occasionally flaring up into frank melodrama.

There is a touch of Conrad, a somewhat similar intricacy
and solemn romanticism." Criticizes Hutchinson's "unremit-
ting solemnity" towards Wild.

S.390.   L.P. Hartley, The Observer (March 3, 1935).
Novelist's convictions triumph over the story's improbability.
Novel "shows literary and imaginative power of a high order."

S.391.   John Chamberlain, New York Times (March 5, 1935).
The unfashionableness of "heroic literature." "The novelist
of idealism always risks the titters of a skeptical audience."
Hutchinson undeterred "by the high mortality of idealism in
modern fiction," but the foundations of the novel are flim-
sier than those of Man's Fate or Lord Jim. "The element of
coincidence ... constitutes the one false note in an other-
wise convincing book of high gallantry," and reviewer objects to the hint that Greta was always "fated" to marry Wild.
"In his efforts to be idealistic, Mr Hutchinson has been a
little too easily romantic." Best writing in the novel is
"evoked by the moods of nature."

SHINING SCABBARD

S.392.   Pamela Hansford Johnson, Liverpool Post (September 30,
1936).
"An exceptionally fine book, so surely conceived, so remarkably executed, that it should take its place, not only among
the novels of the year, but of the century." Hutchinson
"writes in English, but he thinks in French."

S.393.   J.B. Priestley, Star (October 23, 1936).
"That he is a born novelist, a genuine creator, I have no
doubt whatever." Disappointed that the subject of the novel
insufficiently important, not immediately significant. "Here we
have a real creative writer and we must cherish him."
Praises Hutchinson's power of penetrating alien worlds in
all his novels to date.

S.394.   William Lyon Phelps, Book-of-the-Month Club News (December 1936), 3.
Predicts that before forty Hutchinson "will everywhere be
recognized as one of the leading living novelists." The best
Anglo-Saxon portrait of a French family since James' The
American. Hutchinson seems to have "transformed his nationality." Novel shows the utter devastation of war. Notes
the "illuminating spiritual force" in Hutchinson's novels.

S.395.   Wilson Follett, Saturday Review (December 26, 1936).
Most of the characters "controlled by neurotic impulses and
delusions ... mad folk who provoke occasional suspicion of

sanity." The skill with which Hutchinson gradually builds
up "the atmosphere of madness." Severin's great guilt indicated in his treatment of Armand. Severin family is a
"microcosm of a nation's madness in a world going out of its
head."

S.396.   Edith H. Walton, New York Times (December 27, 1936).
Hutchinson's remarkable ability to assimilate a foreign spirit,
so that the novel reads as if it were a translation. Somber
theme but the novel is told with a bizarre, exuberant humor. The Severins symbolize the crumbling of the old world.
The characters more important than the plot. Novel is flam-
boyant and exaggerated, burlesque and macabre, but "so
startlingly alive that criticism of this sort seems just a little
irrelevant." "A strange, fantastic, irresistible novel."

S.397.   Alfred Kazin, New York Herald Tribune Books (December
27, 1936).
A solid, old-fashioned novel of character, illuminating the
whole society because of the detail with which a part has
been drawn. Hutchinson's characters are rigid, immobile,
but they have the life of those who live in a state of sus-
pension. Not a great novel, though "a model of craftsman-
ship." Is very much a modelled and literary novel, a competent rewriting of earlier realism. "There is a preciseness
about the work, the tidiness of an exact scheme and a quiet
competence, that recalls the faintly glamorous day when the
object was everything in fiction, and every detail, every
grouping, was a tool and not an adornment." Hutchinson's
novel exemplifies a theme, but fails to make it suggest any
universality.

S.398.   Gillian Tindall, New Statesman (June 21, 1968).
The subject is too narrow, the detail "stifling" but "the appalling, musty atmosphere of les gens biens on their uppers
is beautifully conveyed." The title is awful and Church's
introduction to the Duckworth edition "fulsome."

TESTAMENT

S.399.   C. Day Lewis, Book Society News (September 1938), 7-8.
Welcomes a novel "in the grand manner, in the manner of
the great Russian novelists with whom Mr Hutchinson" invites comparison. "A book of extraordinary richness and
diversity," with characters solid and deeply realized. But
the novel, unlike Shining Scabbard, has certain structural
flaws: "the development of the plot is in places clogged by
the weight of detail; the escape of the hero and his family
from revolutionary Russia at the end is slightly touched with
melodrama." Still Hutchinson "is one of the two living Eng-

lish novelists certain to survive." Sees Otraveskov as novel's "hero" and Scheffler's career as "main sub-plot." Latter "a saint in the old Russian manner--the kind of man who,
in spite of his great intelligence and humour, is fated to be
destroyed by the logic of his own uncompromising character,
by the intensity of his private dream." Notes that the Revolution is seen through Otraveskov, whose limited sympathy
makes him blind to the ideals of the Left. Admires the way
Hutchinson has imposed "the novelist's order" on political
chaos.

S.400. The Times Literary Supplement (September 3, 1938).
Sees Hutchinson as essentially a writer of "adventure stories," but he is too much fascinated "by the pleasures of
abundance" and the novel should have been cut. It is best
when Hutchinson concentrates upon action (e.g., the visit to
Anton's cell), but elsewhere the narrative is overloaded with
detail.

S.401. Ralph Straus, Sunday Times (September 4, 1938).
"Stuff here which comes near to greatness." Not too long,
the reader finally sees, because so much must be told if we
are to understand the tragedy. Magnificent scenes and characterization. "There is, indeed, real grandeur here--gran-
deur and beauty as well."

S.402. Frank Swinnerton, The Observer (September 4, 1938).
"Testament is by the highest standards a very important
novel indeed." "An overwhelming picture of life in Russia
... enthralling ... has an irresistible excitingness." Novel
takes us deeply into the minds of Russians and the place.
Novelist's "perfect accord with his imagined Russian narrator." Main reservation is that character of Scheffler loses
definition in middle of the novel. But in general, Hutchinson
is "recording the real in the manner of a master." Concludes
that he "is unquestionably, among modern novelists, in the
very highest class, and good enough to make most of his
contemporaries appear trivial."

S.403. Phyllis Bentley, Yorkshire Post (September 7, 1938).
Prefers Testament to Malraux' Days of Hope, published in
the same week, because former is the story of specific individuals, whereas Days of Hope was written on 'totalitarian'
lines, and individuals are forgotten. Likens Testament to
Zweig's Grischa. Finds it too long, but admires Hutchinson's
magnanimity.

S.404. Sean O'Faolain, John O'London's Weekly (September 9, 1938).
Admires the novel for its scope and for Hutchinson's commit-
ment to individuals, his belief that "the personal truth of an
honest individual is the sweetest truth on earth," but finds

the novel too undirected. The central characters are "symbols of the power of men and women to live and die by the deepest truth of their own selves." The significance finally emerged but it was not "pursued" through the novel, being instead "placed" at the end, too explicitly and overtly.

S.405. Wilfred Gibson, Manchester Guardian (September 9, 1938).
Discovery of Hutchinson as "a fresh source of spiritual nourishment and invigoration." Feels the novel is too long and it would have been even more powerful if cut. Novel's aims divided; it would have been better if Otraveskov had been less fully developed. Hutchinson's "entire absorption and assimilation" of an alien culture is an extraordinary feat. The novel is charged with spiritual exaltation; Hutchinson's "quiet exposition of the significance of spiritual values."

S.406. Kate O'Brien, Spectator (September 9, 1938).
Novel "a victory of imagination" because an English novelist has written "a Russian novel." Testament has "the goodwill of those who care for the art of fiction and deplore its present-day confusion and exploitation." It is "exhaustive, patient and true even in defect." Sees these as Hutchinson's wordiness, heavy-handedness and sentimentality. Scheffler sometimes seems too wooden and distant in the early part of the novel, before his trial and death. Theme is the triumph of greatness over confusion, injustice and mutilation. Makes the point that the English-speaking world is likely to distrust sustained seriousness such as Hutchinson's portrayal of Scheffler. The novelist makes no allowance for English readership. "He is non-English in his bold indifference to variation of tone, and he is Russian in that comedy is not, for him, a property of tragedy, but something else, passed on the way, or carried absent-mindedly." He is not afraid either of monotony or intensity. "An immense tale of sorrow, love, endurance, agony and despair."

S.407. V.S. Pritchett, Bystander (September 14, 1938).
Hutchinson lacks any sense of proportion: the novel could have been a third the length. Testament talented but "monumentally unoriginal." Scheffler is Prince Myshkin "in a Quakerish Catholic disguise." Hutchinson's fecundity is self-defeating. "What a good adventure story ... this would have been without the padding."

S.408. Desmond Shawe-Taylor, New Statesman (September 17, 1938).
Hutchinson satisfies a primitive human love of good narrative, but also has a modern understanding of man's spiritual predicament. His noble theme is the conflict of authority and conscience. Flaws: style is solid rather than imaginative; lacks variation in pace; narrator's story is intrusive. But the whole design is skilled, assured, inventive.

S.409. D.A. Traversi, The Tablet (September 24, 1938).
Hutchinson is at his best in telling a plain story of action;
Scheffler's character is too big for him to handle. "A character strong enough to stand out against this vast, shifting
background would have to be conceived with great intellectual
subtlety and immense emotional conviction; to say that Testament does not show these qualities in adequate measure is
merely to deny it a comparable status to, say, War and
Peace." Hutchinson inspired by Dostoyevski's Prince Myshkin
in creating Scheffler, but the latter "is rather a stock character than the outcome of deep personal interests in the author." Scheffler is swallowed up by the complex events of
the novel. "His convictions remain a little abstract and re-
mote." Testament is "a very competent, a very readable,
but in no sense a great novel."

S.410. Edwin Muir, The Listener (September 29, 1938).
A novel of enormous interest despite its flaws (spiritual melodrama, political partiality, sentimental love scenes). "The
religious part of the story is the weakest; but its feeling
for character and incident and its dramatic power are very
unusual; and for imaginative excitement it probably sur-
passes any novel that has appeared for a considerable time."

S.411. Douglas Goldring, Palestine Post (Jerusalem) (October 2,
1938).
The length of the novel is justified. "An astonishing
achievement."

S.412. Pamela Hansford Johnson, Liverpool Post (October 12, 1938).
Describes Hutchinson as "a literary chameleon of overwhelming talents." Admires novel greatly, but believes it too
long.

S.413. John Cournos, New York Times Book Review (October 23,
1938).
Hutchinson's success in creating "human beings against a
background of war and revolution, human beings who remain human entities, personalities to the end." Praises the
relationship both of characters to the background, and of
character to character. An intensely human story, with at
least four memorable characters. Summarizes novel: first
part, destruction; second part, "reclamation." Compares it
with A Tale of Two Cities.

S.414. Alfred Kazin, New York Herald Tribune (October 23, 1938).
Hutchinson's "amazing virtuoso's gift, his aptitude for running over European boundary lines, for seizing a stranger's
speech, for binding himself to the world's occupation."
This requires sympathy as well as the power of impersona-
tion. His remarkable understanding of Russia. Otraveskov

and Scheffler are portrayed with great success, but the novelist is less effective when writing about the peasants "because he does not care enough" for them.

S.415.   Clifton Fadiman, New Yorker (October 29, 1938).
Hutchinson's "hypertrophy of talent"--he writes too easily and invents too copiously. Unlike Tolstoy, the emotional effect is scattered by the novel's detail and density. The novelist's talents should be sieved.

S.416.   Sir Hugh Walpole, Daily Sketch (November 12, 1938).
"Quite the most promising of the younger novelists in England." Hutchinson's virtues are his creation of character and his spiritual integrity.

S.417.   Frank Swinnerton, "I Admire The Heroic," John O'London's Weekly (January 10, 1941).
He envies Hutchinson his courage in attempting a large canvas and a great theme.

S.418.   Richard Church, Country Life (August 29, 1963).
"One lives rather than reads his books." Compares Testament with War and Peace: "both books are testaments of compassion, mankind's greatest achievement, on which we have founded all religions."

S.419.   Robert Taubman, New Statesman (December 20, 1963).
Testament has moral seriousness, but lacks "particular insights." Its meaning is always large and figurative and "doesn't arise from any fine particular life in the novel, but imposes a rhetoric of its own." Concludes that "Mr Hutchinson is a vague novelist."

THE FIRE AND THE WOOD

S.420.   C. Day Lewis, Book Society News (June 1940).
The novel's successful features are its portrait of genius in action and of woman's love in action. Its theme is the "struggle of the puny human spirit against gigantic material obstacles."

S.421.   Frank Swinnerton, The Observer (June 9, 1940).
A very good novel, if not quite as good as his best. "The book is dramatic, alive, rich in striking contrasts ... and lambent with truly humane humour. It is not overwhelming, as Testament was; but it is by the same author, a real novelist of superlative gifts."

S.422.   Pamela Hansford Johnson, Liverpool Post (June 12, 1940).
Hutchinson always appears to be "playing every front-rank

writer in Europe," and "this protean brilliance" prevents him from becoming a great novelist. Here he writes of Germany like a German, but the reviewer wishes Hutchinson would write in his own manner.

S.423. Richard Church, John O'London's Weekly (June 14, 1940). Courageous choice of theme and the thoroughness of Hutchinson's exploration of this theme. The novelist's objectivity increases the power of the horror. "The two themes, the abnormality of the sick body reflecting that of the sick society, are admirably worked out. But they make a terrible book."

S.424. The Times Literary Supplement (June 15, 1940). A fine portrait of Josef, but the story is too uneven with "too much insignificant detail, more particularly of the medical or clinical sort." The effusive poetry of Minna's diaries and delirium "strikes a note of uncomfortable artifice." Concludes that "the level of imagination on which he works is at present too variable to allow him to make the best use of" his narrative gifts.

S.425. Edward Sackville-West, New Statesman (June 15, 1940). Hutchinson is "the most considerable English novelist of his age," but finds this novel a disappointment. Divides novelists into those whose novels are exquisite explorations of the backwaters of life (Flaubert, Turgenev, James, Proust, Joyce, Woolf); and those who write about the "mainstream" of life (Dickens, Balzac), with breadth, pace and vitality. Hutchinson is placed in the second category: "Mr Hutchinson is, with Jules Romains, the only novelist now writing ... to possess the scope, the vigour, the breadth and the extravagant ability of the great nineteenth-century figures." His "multitudinous imagination" enables him to be "prodigal of his resources," yet this is a disappointing novel, a hurried repeat of Testament, with the central relationship marred by sentimentality. The Nazi theme, too, reviewer argues, is particularly inopportune in the summer of 1940. (The Fire and The Wood was published in the same week as Dunkirk.)

S.426. Hugh Walpole, Daily Sketch (June 24, 1940). Has a high opinion of Hutchinson, though his faults are "confused narrative and an inability to select significant detail." This novel suffers from the latter, the detail in the novel being brilliant, but heavy and clogging. Despite this it "is beyond and above most contemporary fiction."

S.427. Edwin Muir, The Listener (June 27, 1940). "A religious writer with a purgatorial imagination; he is concerned mainly with two things: the soul's salvation and the body's suffering." A slick, professional rewriting of Testa-

ment. No "conventional social feeling" in Hutchinson's novels, which are above and below normal life. The dangers
in this form of fiction are sentimentality and melodrama.

S.428.   V.S. Pritchett, The Bystander (July 10, 1940).
A chameleon novelist, here passing as a German except for
his "ingenious moral preoccupation such as might tease an
English clergyman." His talent is "phenomenally ingenious.
In its realism and its development of the situation The Fire
and The Wood is highly original and humane; yet its sources
appear to be completely derivative."

S.429.   George Dangerfield, Saturday Review of Literature (August
31, 1940).
Hutchinson's honorable failure in trying to understand Nazism mars the second half of the novel. The first half is
"a fine example of the dramatic interplay of unpretentious
incident and minute characterization." In the second half
Hutchinson seems so appalled by the images of the Nazis
that he too is keen to escape. The novel is "a distinguished
and touching" failure.

S.430.   C.S. Forester, New York Herald Tribune (September 1,
1940).
Hutchinson has a powerful and logical imagination and he is
a fine storyteller. Has simple, "nervous" style. But the
reviewer is still unable to account for the power of the novel: "the whole gives an extraordinary impression of reality,
along with ... elusive charm."

S.431.   John Cournos, New York Times Book Review (September 1,
1940).
A "deeply felt story, powerful in its writing and passionate
in its truth," though not as good as Testament. Hutchinson's interest is "revealing the effects revolutions have on
the psyche of fine, sensitive souls, indifferent to them, but
caught in their meshes."

S.432.   Martin Seymour-Smith, Scotsman (July 18, 1970).
The novel is close to the work of Dornford Yates, but is
readable and has integrity.

S.433.   Clive Jordan, New Statesman (July 24, 1970).
"The brush strokes are broad and the emotions conventional,
but the story convinces until, with the couple's escape, it
lapses into slapdash melodrama."

INTERIM

S.434.   The Times Literary Supplement (March 31, 1945).

Reviewer respects and admires Hutchinson, but is unmoved
by his work. Like earlier novels, Interim "exhibits the author's grave, intellectualized turn of speech, his partiality
for remarkable characters and varieties of experience, and
his fondness for enunciating truths of one sort or another,
often truths most acutely perceived, in what may be thought
too explicit a fashion." Admires the novelist's seriousness
and ability, but fears his "creative gesture" is "somewhat
too large," his philosophy "a shade stilted." This novel
lacks "emotional spontaneity," the novel is too contrived.
In its discovery of saintliness Interim "always rather larger
than life."

S.435. Howard Spring, Country Life (April 13, 1945).
The spiritual teaching is all done by implication. The message is that Quindle is invulnerable. The novel is "short
but perfect." Hutchinson "is confirmed as one of the few
significant novelists of our day."

S.436. Philip Toynbee, New Statesman (April 14, 1945).
Interim is "positively and virulently vulgar," and dreadfully
representative of the "official opposition" to modern materi-
alism, a "mélange of platitude and philistinism, shallow ...
fundamentally untruthful ... kitsch."

S.437. Richard Church, John O'London's Weekly (April 20, 1945).
Compares Hutchinson with Conrad, for he too has "spiritual
individuality." Finds Interim "desperately moving." It is
one of Hutchinson's best works, because of its shortness
and lack of detail. The novel's "lyrical agony." Hutchinson's central belief is in man's free will.

S.438. Edwin Muir, The Listener (April 26, 1945).
The "high temperature" of Hutchinson's style suits his usual
violent and catastrophic themes, but is unfitted to the material of this novel. "The reader finds himself waiting des-
pairingly for a sentence naturally turned and with a quiet
fall." Also marred by the facetiousness of the dialogue,
but reviewer finds the ending of the novel more direct and
appealing.

S.439. Marguerite Young, New York Times (May 13, 1945).
The difficulty of describing this novel, which evades definition. "For Mr Hutchinson, it may be, life is made up of
disparities, fragments, disrelations." "There is almost no
principle of coherence, no informative vision, other than ...
the story is told by a single narrator." But the narrator
himself is fragmentary, detached. Hutchinson is a novelist
interested in externals only: "a dry-as-dust realist." No
singularity of vision or intention in the novel. The narrator's mental limitations. The one certitude in Interim is
"monotony and slow disintegration into death."

S.440.   Walter Allen, Time and Tide (June 2, 1945).
         Feels distaste for the novel. Shoddy presentation of a seri-
         ous subject. Intolerably facetious and "very vulgar."

ELEPHANT AND CASTLE

S.441.   Clifton Fadiman, Book-of-the-Month Club News (January
         1949).
         "Elephant and Castle is at once a melodrama of crime and
         punishment; a psychological study of a woman who is both
         appealing and appalling; a social novel in which are juxta-
         posed and contrasted two worlds--London's rarefied gentry
         and its swarming, murky East End; a portrait gallery of
         low-life grotesques, Hogarthian in humor and in power; and,
         finally, a Christian novel, embodying the ancient and en-
         during gospel of love." The successor to Dickens and Bal-
         zac, though faulted by melodrama and over-complication.
         Hutchinson's ability to create character "in the grand and
         simple manner of the great nineteenth-century novelists."

S.442.   John Cournos, New York Sun (January 27, 1949).
         London itself is perhaps the most important of all Hutchin-
         son's characters. Not "Dickensian," because the novel is
         a modern, post-Freudian nightmare.

S.443.   Ivor Brown, New York Times Book Review (January 30,
         1949).
         The novel masterfully survives all its handicaps and limita-
         tions. Hutchinson's "penetrative eye which drives into the
         odd corners of the soul." Criticizes complex and irritating
         narrative, the mixture of first and third persons. Finds in-
         credible Armorel's degradation. Argues that Hutchinson's
         point is that "London will in the end corrupt anyone."
         Novel is superbly moving with passages (childbirth or the
         ending) that are unbearably poignant.

S.444.   Sean O'Faolain, The Listener (April 7, 1949).
         Feels respect and caution towards Hutchinson, "probably one
         of those writers whom it will take a considerable passage of
         time to measure." The novel is "impressive and puzzling,"
         apparently without formal design. Such a sprawling novel
         can only be justified by its "matter," but the reviewer is
         flummoxed by the psychology of Hutchinson's characters,
         who are presented with the morbidity of Ibsen or Dreiser.
         Reviewer feels out of his depth with the unpredictable ac-
         tions of Armorel and Gian. The effect of this couple and of
         Trevon and Elizabeth is that one feels "in the realm rather
         of the alienist than the novelist." Elephant and Castle ex-
         plains the crime in rational terms but fails to emphasize
         "the awe of the mystery." Summary: the novel is impres-
         sive but not as profound as Testament.

S.445.   John Betjeman, Daily Herald (April 27, 1949).
         The novel's aim is to show that the inarticulate are deeper
         and braver than the glib.

S.446.   Richard Church, John O'London's Weekly (April 29, 1949).
         The basic improbability of the novel, which the reader yet
         finally accepts. Respects novel for its vast scale and the
         novelist's fecundity, which he compares with Dickens'. In
         effect it is a "profound moral essay" on spiritual pride and
         self-righteousness. Concludes that it is a great book.

S.447.   J.W. Lambert, Manchester Daily Despatch (April 29, 1949).
         Not a complete success, but novel has one finely drawn
         character, Gian, though Armorel is unbelievable. "Here
         are many fine things, but in drawing with such careless
         prodigality upon romance and reality he has imperilled not
         merely the book's unity, which doesn't matter, but also its
         fundamental sincerity, which does."

S.448.   Pamela Hansford Johnson, Daily Telegraph (April 29, 1949).
         Places Hutchinson in the tradition of Dickens, Trollope and
         Tolstoy, the large nineteenth-century novelists who treat
         the major experiences of human life. But she finds this
         novel "wrong at the core," because the central situation,
         the marriage, was "fabricated." Hutchinson lacks "aesthetic
         tact."

S.449.   Philip Toynbee, New Statesman (April 30, 1949).
         Certain that Hutchinson won't survive because, unlike Dos-
         toyevski, he hasn't contributed to our inheritance. Com-
         ments, after two quotes, that "the texture of Elephant and
         Castle is quite peculiarly displeasing. Mr Hutchinson writes
         with a lush flamboyance which cloys and sickens." His
         Christian intentions are clear enough in his "expansive dis-
         sertation," but he fails to deepen our apprehension of life.
         Characters, places and situations are all grossly "contrived"
         and akin to "any pretentious popular novel of our time."
         Life escapes from the novel and it lacks the "vital reality"
         that Julian Huxley found in it.

S.450.   Michael Sadleir, Sunday Times (May 1, 1949).
         Finds the story unbelievable--"wilful extravagance of style
         and episode makes it a dizzy jumble of surrealism, knock-
         about and verbal intransigence. The tragedy is that the
         extravagance obscures the book's many excellences--Gian
         himself, drawn with consistent care and affection; a dozen
         minor characters; innumerable touches of observation and
         glimpses of the macabre; a lovely tenderness towards small
         helpless things."

S.451.   The Times Literary Supplement (May 6, 1949).

The novel begins to become incredible after the marriage
(e.g., the wedding scene "with its impossible mixture of
classes and burlesque climax"; the grotesque quarrel between the doctors, and Armorel's confinement; Armorel's
decision to send her son to a special school). The novel is
incredible because the novelist has strained his imagination.
"It is this sense of strain which makes Elephant and Castle
so uncomfortable."

S.452. Elizabeth Bowen, Tatler (May 18, 1949).
Realizes that the crime is fictitious. "The guise of circum-
stantiality" gives the novel a firm and lively frame. Triumph
of the novel is in its inevitability. Notes the changes in our
attitude to Armorel--sympathy, admiration, cool respect, out-
rage. Novel had to be long because "its action covers nearly twenty years, its theme is formidable and its exploration
of the soul requires space."

S.453. Alex Comfort, "The Novels of Mr Hutchinson," World Review
(July 1949).
Despite the paralysis of critics Hutchinson is "one of our
most important living writers." He cannot be understood if
we look for "incisiveness ... direct perception, or ... sym-
bolical use of realism." His place in literary history is as
a writer who has attempted to take Naturalism beyond Zola.
Modern writers are faced with extraliterary competition in
naturalism. Hutchinson's solution to the problem of making
the social novel available for art is "stylistic." Like Arnold
Zweig, he thus manages to avoid competing with the sociolo-
gist, because "he employs his style and diction as a trans-
parent but perceptible screen between reader and realism."
Like Zola, Hutchinson avoids the symbolist's selection of
events and persons; secondly, realistic speech "is set in a
prolonged soliloquy by the writer, speaking through the
minds of everyone and everything who moves into the field
of vision." This reverie-technique offends contemporary
critical taste; it is also dangerous in its tendency to drift
into falsity, as in Armorel's dying reverie. Hutchinson succeeds so often because of his use of "real observation to
anchor the drift of comment." "The real scene, then, with
its protective screen of diction, distinguishes this kind of
naturalism." Like Dickens, he has complete grasp of his
material, but the "film of fiction" protects his real material
from reminiscence or reporting. His occasional opacities--
bizarre names, falsity in some reveries or in the reality of
dialogue. Characters are seen with great clarity, but from
outside, from action, speech and event. "The claim which
this book establishes, then, depends on three things--it
has the scale of a major novel, its technique and its observation match that scale, and its total success is uniform enough
to make it comparable with other major work." Hutchinson

is not just a survivor of the school of Galsworthy; but a
major contemporary novelist, a writer of genuine technical
mastery.

S.454.   Stevie Smith, Modern Woman (August 1949).
"This novel touches the heights and depths of human conduct and motive. Absolutely first-rate."

S.455.   Richard Lister, Evening Standard (June 24, 1969).
Thinks the length is justified but that some of the perspec-
tives we are given fail to clarify the relationship. Finds a
"fatal streak of romanticism in his treatment of relationships."
It is implausible that Gian doesn't notice Armorel's wound.
This is all "splendidly operatic, but doesn't strike us as re-
motely conceivable, and so is quite out of tune with the realistic treatment elsewhere."

RECOLLECTION OF A JOURNEY

S.456.   Brian Moore, Montreal Gazette (May 10, 1952).
The novel is about "the ethics of courage" but the Kolbecks'
is a "peculiar inverted" form of patriotism. Recollection of
a Journey has the "sureness of documentary writing."
Moore does not share the novelist's admiration for Julius
who, to him, is little different from the Nazis or Russians.
What purpose is his love of country when unaccompanied by
any love for individuals?

S.457.   Nathan Rothman, Saturday Review of Literature (May 24,
1952).
Recollection's "maudlin inconsequence" because Hutchinson
chose the wrong hero, from lack of a sense of proportion.
Stefanie, "a tiresome and fuzzy-minded bore," is wrong to
believe that the tragedy of Poland was the degradation of
its aristocrats. We are not stirred, because we are asked
to weep, not for the masses but for the lost ancestral es-
tates. How can we weep for the Kolbecks? "The book has
a strange, anachronistic flavor about it. It has the wrong
hero, although the villains are right enough. Its approach
to the recent history that gave it birth is so narrow in
sympathies, and the behavior of the people it champions--
General Kolbeck, his son Victor, his daughter-in-law Stef-
anie--is so often absurd, that one may wonder at the docu-
ments its writer consulted."

S.458.   David Paul, Observer (October 26, 1952).
The difficulty of judging Hutchinson, "this least personal,
least stylish of novelists" because he disappears so completely into the experience he creates. "I doubt whether in all
literature there could be a greater monolith to human misery
and endurance."

S.459. Stephen Spender, The Listener (October 30, 1952).
The novel "a wonderful vindication of the power of the novel
to hold up a mirror to the most confusing events in our
time." Hutchinson "establishes a bridge between our own
lives and those of people who have lived in the worst hell
of our time." The novel blends the realism of L'Education
Sentimentale with Kafkaesque fantasy. Hutchinson's humanity, his ability to break through "the shell of his own personal experience and enter a kind of objective sympathy with
a world wider than himself. He enlarges our sense of what
is meant by others."

S.460. The Times Literary Supplement (October 31, 1952).
The novel has seriousness, irony, impersonality, descriptive
power, but it lacks tenseness and horror: "as a work of
art it is prosaic to the point of dullness." Hutchinson's
inability to individualize characters: only Stefanie has engaged "the imagination of her creator." Praises the ambition
and seriousness of the novel, but argues that Hutchinson
lacks "the imaginative capacity that could transform the factual nightmares of yesterday and today into artistic reality."

S.461. Richard Church, John O'London's Weekly (October 31, 1952).
The "hieratic gravity" with which Hutchinson approaches the
novelist's task, though the reviewer would welcome a lighten-
ing humor. In this novel he writes "with no doctrine, no
political comment, no thesis other than his incorrigible love
for single human beings and the sanctity of their private
lives." Church pays tribute to the fecundity of Hutchinson's
imagination, but wonders if his universe is connected with
experience and the real outside world. The danger is that
he will produce a Salammbô, a lifeless masterpiece. Recollection escapes that fate: it is desperately moving.

S.462. John Betjeman, Daily Telegraph (October 31, 1952).
The narrative is muddling, full of digressions, which weaken
Hutchinson's tragic, thrilling story.

THE STEPMOTHER

S.463. John Betjeman, Daily Telegraph (September 9, 1955).
Unpretentious, competent, concise. Ending is touching and
convincing.

S.464. Norman Shrapnel, Manchester Guardian (September 13, 1955).
Technically first-rate. "Mr Hutchinson is obsessed with the
weight and the deviousness of biography, with the complicated burden that the past imposes on every human life.
His straightforward handling is right. We get a sense of
order and lucidity imposed by the observing mind upon the

stealthy chaos of what people do and say. Few of our novelists match such drive with such equipment."

S.465.   The Times (September 22, 1955).
A novel "conceived and executed in the spirit of humility,"
"stronger and more profound in its exploration of human relationships than at first sight appears." The notion of
Hutchinson as the Clapham Junction signaller who has here
chosen to work on a branch line.

S.466.   The Times Literary Supplement (October 7, 1955).
Contrasts the short, concentrated Stepmother with the "epic"
proportions of Testament and Recollection. Yet there are
similarities as well: the patient unfolding of character; the
range of characters that Hutchinson can realize; "the sense
of modern history (Mr Hutchinson's people are always involved with the world about them.)" The weakness is that
his treatment of Stephen's psychological problem is less impressive than in Testament. "But The Stepmother is a work
of great distinction, the writing as finely fluent as ever, the
English as deliberate and as clean."

S.467.   Stevie Smith, The Observer (October 9, 1955).
Competent, but artificial and contrived.

MARCH THE NINTH

S.468.   Richard Church, The Bookman (October 1957).
"A most impressive novel. It combines brilliant story-telling
with a moral and emotional sensibility that brings the author
into the depths of human oddity and grandeur." Compares
Hutchinson with Conrad--in his 'infrequency' and in "the
poetic overtone, the slightly humorous dignity and tone of
his work, the aloofness due to intense nervous apprehension."
Hutchinson's ability to create minor facts, "the imaginative
creation of circumstantial event and action," is shared with
major novelists such as Fielding, Dickens, Balzac and Dumas.
The novel's moral purpose or symbolism only appears in
recollection, after the excitement of the narrative.

S.469.   Tom Hopkinson, Observer (November 3, 1957).
The story is original and exciting but it appears contrived.
The ending is too neat; Reichenbach feels more English than
Austro-American; the vocabulary is too esoteric; and, most
of all, Hutchinson's "incessant analysis of emotion ... pre-
vents that emotion being communicated as real."

S.470.   Charles Clay, Daily Worker (November 7, 1957).
"A well-written, cleverly contrived novel which, however,
fails to move the reader because its underlying approach to

life is phoney and pretentious." "The character of Zempel-
mark is thoughtfully--and too sympathetically--worked out,
while far less attempt is made to portray imaginatively the
feelings and lives of his victims and their families." The
death at the end "is a piece of grotesque and sickening
sentimentality."

S.471.   Walter Allen, New Statesman (November 9, 1957).
The theme is serious and the story is beautifully composed,
but the novel seems dead because (1) Reichenbach is unbe-
lievable as an Austro-American; he reads like "a nice upper-
class Englishman;" (2) the style is inappropriately literary
and rhetorical. The reviewer quotes Verlaine's comment
about Tennyson: "too noble, too Anglais, and, when he
should have been broken-hearted, had many reminiscences."

S.472.   John Bayley, Spectator (November 15, 1957).
"Mr Hutchinson has always been for me a baffling but oddly
impressive writer. He seems to construct his rigorous and
laborious situation-pieces--queer dilemmas of conscience and
feeling in a vaguely Balkan setting--on the basis recommended by Henry James when he said that after catching a
glimpse in Lyons of a family at dinner one ought to be able
to write a novel about French protestantism. In this study
of a polyglot doctor in Slovenia involved in the fate of a
wounded ex-Nazi, Mr Hutchinson shows an equally splendid
disregard for mere experience and an equally scrupulous
feel for a state of mind. His technique is not abstract--the
calibre of every machine-gun is mentioned--but it is too considered to seem like life to most people."

S.473.   Peter Green, Daily Telegraph (November 15, 1957).
Hutchinson's hesitancy about the novel's purpose. An international thriller, like Buchan and Household? A serious novel about postwar Europe? Hutchinson is a good storyteller,
though Reichenbach's nationality is incredible.

S.474.   The Times Literary Supplement (November 22, 1957).
"A sadly inflated morality, told in terms of an adventure
story." The novel is curiously lifeless. "This seems partly
a result of Mr Hutchinson's ruminative style, which fits badly with accounts of violent action, and partly because his
characters are concerned with mere demonstrations of certain human qualities."

S.475.   Anthony Quinton, London Magazine (February 1958).
Hutchinson has written an excellent thriller in trying to raise
this form to the level of tragedy.

IMAGE OF MY FATHER

S.476. Daniel George, The Bookman (September 1961).
Prophesies that "when someone--as someone surely will--
comes to write about the total oeuvre of R.C. Hutchinson he
will not find it easy to categorize the novels: each is different from its predecessors, all remain uninfluenced by contemporary fashion in fiction. His latest, Image of My Father,
would break away from any pattern a critic was trying to impose." It is a "study of egoism," a "quite remarkable novel."

S.477. Peter Green, Daily Telegraph (October 6, 1961).
At one level it is a Galsworthian novel of wills and inherit-
ances, but the story of Vincent is very un-English, reminiscent of "Mauriac in one of his grimmer moments." The conflict between continental and English mores: "two alien
worlds, crystallised by Vincent's stay with the Selbornes under a pseudonym, is a triumph of shrewd insight and deli-
cate irony." A deeply impressive novel.

S.478. The Times Literary Supplement (October 6, 1961).
An impressive, large-scale novel. Interesting and professional, though the ending is "a not altogether convincing
surprise."

S.479. Richard Church, Country Life (October 12, 1961).
A strange, haunting tale. Vincent's return to Germaine is
masochistic and unconvincing, because "it involves too much
spiritual damage to its perpetrators." But the novel is a
powerful account of Vincent's "adventure in hell ... the dark
night of the soul."

S.480. Margaret Wilson, Stafford Newsletter (December 23, 1961).
Hutchinson is an excellent storyteller, though the narrative
is always of secondary interest. Three strands of the past
constitute the plot: Vincent's birth, marriage and war experience. The method of narration is a mixture of probing
into the past, reflecting on the present, and anticipating the
future. The novel's first section is the short "Prologue."
Vincent's search for his identity is accompanied by four
women. At the end he finds self-knowledge. "This self-
knowledge is accompanied by such charity and compassion
that he ceases to seek anything for himself. The true good,
as Hutchinson sees it, comes only through self-sacrifice."
The contrast between the women: sensual Germaine/intelli-
gent Ruth. Both mothers are clever and charming, "but,
whereas Lucille is limited in her sympathies and not too
scrupulous, Marie-Christine has perfect integrity and an all-
embracing compassion."

S.481. Anthony Burgess, Yorkshire Post (December 28, 1961).
"A classic study of egotism."

S.482. Charles Poore, New York Times (January 4, 1962).
"The Inheritor ... is a novel about the natural history of a
man called Selborne." Criticizes it because it is "over-
furnished" (Willa Cather) ... scenes are stretched out too
long. Also a lavish use of coincidence.

S.483. Aileen Pippett, Saturday Review (January 13, 1962).
"Meticulously plotted, rational and convincing at every stage,
though its end leaves many doubts." Hutchinson is an
"eminently civilized man who can chart a course to sanity
through violence, madness and despair. His characters never dissolve in sentimentality because he accepts the limits
imposed by inheritance and environment on their freedom
to change their natures. This basic rationality makes his
monsters credible and his saints sympathetic." Also praises
Hutchinson's ability to orchestrate human voices and his
genuine liking for women.

A CHILD POSSESSED

S.484. Stephen Wall, The Listener (September 24, 1964).
"The opportunities for sentiment are resisted by the intelligence with which Mr Hutchinson conducts the story, but
there is a residual novelletishness in the material which he
is not able entirely to overcome; there is also rather too
much local French colour. A Child Possessed is moving because one cannot but respond to the author's humanity, but
the intention is rather under-cut by the facility of the writing."

S.485. Arthur Calder-Marshall, Financial Times (September 24, 1964).
"R.C. Hutchinson is the most underrated novelist of our
time. He has the high seriousness to which Charles Morgan
pretended. He disregards fashion. He refuses to repeat in
each book the success of others. His novels are adventures
into wildernesses of the spirit where the going is rough and
even paths blazed in the past are overgrown with secondary
scrub." Stepan reminds us of Dostoyevski's The Idiot and
the philosophical discussions are reminiscent of the same
novelist, but the relation of Stepan and Eugénie "is treated
with splendid unsentimentality." The novel "is a fine, chal-
lenging consideration of the inviolability of human personality."

S.486. Jocelyn Brooke, Spectator (September 25, 1964).
Describes Stepan as "a sort of Dostoyevskian Holy Fool."
Hutchinson's concern with moral issues places him in F.R.
Leavis' "Great Tradition," relates him "far more closely than
Lawrence, to George Eliot, James and Conrad."

S.487.   Walter Allen, Daily Telegraph (October 1, 1964).
         A terrifying situation explored without sentimentality or sen-
         sationalism. But the novel is too "literary," with Stepan
         coming from Dostoyevski.

S.488.   The Times Literary Supplement (October 1, 1964).
         The novel's effect is "muffled" because of the "extremely
         leisurely and dated manner" in which it is told. Several in-
         cidents and characters are unnecessary. The moral is un-
         impeachable, but it could have been put more succinctly.

S.489.   R.G.G. Price, Punch (October 7, 1964).
         Hutchinson is working in a Victorian narrative tradition,
         "deliberate, elaborate, inventive." His strength is with the
         episode, but this always has a place in the pattern. This
         novel avoids sentimentality and the schematic. Everything in
         it is relevant.

S.490.   Richard Church, Country Life (October 22, 1964).
         All Hutchinson's novels share "the ability to express a pur-
         pose and a philosophy, not by means of argument and com-
         ment, but by the creation of facts." At the end of this nov-
         el "marital love [is] explored to its depth and set up as a
         lasting refuge, by a moral philosopher whose work remains
         four-square and monumental."

JOHANNA AT DAYBREAK

S.491.   Norman Shrapnel, The Guardian (May 2, 1969).
         Novel is "elaborate, quietly strong, immediately distinctive
         in the heavily built-up field of war-guilt fiction." "A grave
         and deeply absorbed novel, so well modulated as to be never
         for a moment heavy or sententious."

S.492.   James Fenton, New Statesman (May 2, 1969).
         The theme of "this excellent novel" is "the sense of respon-
         sibility." "The wrongdoers and the wronged are all sub-
         jected to the same critical analysis, and no one is found to
         belong wholly to either category." It is "most remarkable
         on sheer technical grounds, for its handling of a given true
         [sic] story so that there is no otiose material, and for the
         gradual revelation of the truth through the uncertain and
         ambiguous point of view of the narrator, which develops
         through stages of fear, isolation, resignation and despair
         towards something verging on hope."

S.493.   R.G.G. Price, Punch (May 7, 1969).
         "A Trollope with Europe for his base, a very English Thomas
         Mann, he deceptively screens his contemporary awareness by
         his mastery of fictional techniques developed by his prede-

cessors. He tells a story faultlessly, sets his scenes amply, is not afraid of the pathetic as well as the tragic, knows a lot about the world during this century and, above all, invents, invents, invents." This novel's "bleak stoicism is always relieved by [Hutchinson's] loving knowledge of a surviving world."

S.494. Richard Church, Country Life (June 12, 1969).
Hutchinson reinstates the novel as a major literary form, "presenting, with literary skill, moral authority and psychological insight, a commentary on contemporary life that is inescapable." His work "has a singleness of purpose, each book adding, with increasing clarity and directness, to the exploration of the author's faith in the final authority of conscience over the individual character of men and women, and its enlargement to the moral, political and religious life of society." Hutchinson does not preach, he tells a story, creating facts which "have the semblance of minute actuality." His novels show the "triumph of conscience." He is a "mystic, powerful and agonised" and a humorist as well. The impressive simplicity and permanence of Hutchinson's work.

S.495. The Times Literary Supplement (June 19, 1969).
"Mr Hutchinson's fictions stretch away behind him through three decades, spaced out like massive and stately mansions along some private avenue where nobody walks but he. They are spacious, constructed by a dedicated craftsman quick to reject anything shoddy or faked, and are all immediately recognizable as the work of the same hand." Hutchinson's technique is equal to the ambitious design of Johanna. His gift for characterization and his skill at evoking the mood of the period. Yet his failing is the monotony of his style-- "the hypnotic sameness about Mr Hutchinson's prose rhythms."

S.496. Bernice Rubens, Jewish Chronicle (August 15, 1969).
A very powerful novel, though Hutchinson himself is a non-Jewish reporter. "A moving and indignant tale." Johanna is not a "nice" woman, but the novelist imbues her with "the touch of dignity." The novel is "a powerful and beautifully written plea for our tolerance."

S.497. Gilbert Highet, Book-of-the-Month Club News (November 1969).
Hutchinson's "copious and thoughtful mind." His interest in individuals who rise again after being beaten by totalitarianism and their own weaknesses. This novel's "profound sympathy for suffering." Criticizes Hutchinson for using Johanna as point of view: it is artificial that a woman who has already discovered her past should at the beginning have to pretend to be mistaken. "It would have been clearer, though less intimate, if the tale had been told by some-

one else, such as a sympathetic doctor who observed it from without."

S.498.   Martin Levin, New York Times (November 2, 1969).
The nineteenth-century formality of Hutchinson's style is set against the modernity of his theme, "the problem of individual responsibility and guilt in the context of mass criminality."

ORIGINS OF CATHLEEN

S.499.   Norman Shrapnel, The Guardian (September 9, 1971).
"A likeable, offbeat novel though its modes are not successfully merged." Beginning is a kind of "affectionate parody of autobiographical childhood." The mixture of buffoonery and tragedy is not quite successful.

S.500.   Susan Hill, New Statesman (September 10, 1971).
Hutchinson is "a direct and unashamed descendant of the nineteenth-century narrative tradition, and his new book is many-layered, long, leisurely--a family saga full of careful detail." "Full of warmth and good humour, comforting and truthful--sentimental at the core perhaps, but a good example of its author's solid, if unfashionable, worth."

S.501.   Richard Church, Country Life (December 2, 1971).
"A wild farce" but "the procession of oddities and clowns ... turns out to be the human wolf-pack gleefully escorting a saint to his execution." Sees Hutchinson as basically a tragic writer, producing "tragic works of a profound and severe compassion," a tragedian who has here written a "wildly hilarious farce."

RISING

S.502.   Janice Elliott, Sunday Telegraph (September 5, 1976).
"Some readers may find this South American epic, set at the turn of the century, heavy going. Admirers will recognise with pleasure this writer's painstaking characterisation, meticulous realism and humanity."

S.503.   Jill Neville, Sunday Times (September 5, 1976).
"Hutchinson's tapestry is enormous and somewhat over-detailed, even tedious at times; his time is early twentieth century, his characters often inscrutable even to themselves, but their interaction, their combustions of personality and slower upheavals on the deepest levels lift this book high above the usual historical novel."

S.504. Isabel Quigly, Financial Times (September 9, 1976).
"An impressive novel, large-scale, slow-moving, sonorous,
with a strong, occasionally archaic style and a moving use
of landscape and the unfamiliar patterns of life in a feudal
South America early this century."

S.505. S. Kennedy, The Times Literary Supplement (September 10,
1976).
"The nightmarish journey across rivers and mountains gives
the novel a mythic proportion, but although the confrontation
with Papac, which transforms Sabino physically and spiritual-
ly, takes place in a dreamlike state, it is firmly rooted in
reality. By a gloriously rich use of language (occasionally
giving way to a self-conscious obscurantism), Mr Hutchinson
meticulously creates a whole society and topography." The
lack of a final chapter produces a sense of anticlimax.
Hutchinson's good characters (Yupanqui, Patricio, Marta)
not as interesting as the ambiguous, such as the Bishop.
"There is no doubting the area of his deepest concern--wit-
ness his searing indictment of the spiritual deprivation of
poverty--but it is his portrayal of the rich, whose redemption
has the more painfullyto be worked out, which, blending
irony with compassion, fully engages his understanding and
talent."

S.506. Mary Cosh, Northern Echo (September 16, 1976).
"The stature of this book is difficult to convey in so few
words, with its multi-dimensional grasp of the power of the
mind for good or ill, or of the will for bodily endurance;
and its poet's apprehension of the beauties and cruelties of
terrestrial wilderness, and the lapidary quality of observed
detail. Though one might carp at longeurs, this is a major work from a major author."

S.507. Neil Jillett, The Herald (USA) (November 25, 1976).
"A strange, mystifying, lumbering novel." Hutchinson re-
sembles Conrad in his efforts to give moral force to a story
of violent action. He writes with wordy, discursive care,
as if testing the strengths and complexities of a language
not his own. "At its best Rising is a powerful novel, both
as drama and moral fable. Page after page grips the attention. At other times its portentousness degenerates into
preachy pomposity: the tapestry of story and sermon become tediously tangled."

S.508. Mervyn Horder, PEN Club Bulletin (November 1976).
"A work of unflagging splendour." Praises the "power and
ingenuity with which the whole plot is orchestrated, the
searching, warm-hearted analysis of each character ... the
grandeur of the philosophy, positively Christian as the author
was himself, which illuminates the tale." Notes that the novel was the only one Hutchinson based on his own travels.

Suggests two reasons for his lack of wide recognition: his personal modesty; and the great length and complexity of his novels.

T.   Reviews of Short Stories

"A Photograph of Mrs Austin"

T.509.   John O'London's Weekly (October 28, 1938).
"An excellent example of what clever handling can do for a rather ordinary theme."

"Crossroads"

T.510.   The Times Literary Supplement (November 20, 1948).
"R.C. Hutchinson makes us shudder at ruthlessness more violently than over any glimpse of the supernatural or record of physical tortures."

T.511.   Richard Lister, New Statesman (December 4, 1948).
"A story that almost persuades me to re-apply for membership in the select club of his admirers."

"All in the Day"

T.512.   Reginald Moore, Time and Tide (January 2, 1954).
A story that "incises the callous military skin and draws a few drops of warm blood."

"How I Rose to Be an Australian Shoeshine Boy"

T.513.   Elizabeth Jennings, The Spectator (December 28, 1956).
A "trick story," with a "contrived or surprise" ending which bears little "relation to human behaviour."

U.   Reviews of PAIFORCE

U.514.   Glasgow Herald (January 28, 1949).
Notes that this is the official "story," not the official "history." Hence it has plenty of illustrations and maps. "The style too has the characteristic metallic glitter, distributing praise so voluminous and general as to take the edge off most of it except the genuinely emotional tribute at the end to the British soldier. If it recalls Fortescue's peroration it

is none the worse for that." "The story is told briefly and
well and, rightly in a work of this kind, contains much that
is personal. If it is not a monumental history it is a worthy
tribute to a gallant, hard-working, and too often forgotten
force."

U.515.   The Times (January 29, 1949).
"The manner, at once romantic and arch, rather reminiscent
of Kipling in less happy moments, comes almost as a shock
today, though it is that of publications with incredible cir-
culations during and just after the war."

U.516.   J.R.D., Yorkshire Evening Post (February 11, 1949).
Reviewer recalls that it was he who, while with Paiforce,
had the task of persuading the Army, the Ministry of Information and the Treasury that the story should be written.
Criticizes the book because Hutchinson "does not get below
the level of the brasshats and brigadiers in assessing all
that happened. As a result, his book lacks what can only
be called 'human interest.'"

U.517.   The Listener (March 24, 1949).
"A belated record of great services, well illustrated and
plainly--on occasion eloquently--written."

V.   Reviews of LAST TRAIN SOUTH

V.518.   E.P.M., News Chronicle (August 12, 1938).
"A whirl of activity about an axis of nothingness." Blames
Basil Dean (who seems "as a director to be reaching a sort
of second childishness which mistakes noise for drama") for
transforming any meaning in the play to "a blurred meaning-
lessness by a bustle of purposeless action."

V.519.   [Charles Morgan], The Times (August 12, 1938).
The play lacked coherence, direction and form. "The stage
is continuously active, but seldom alive with the life of sympathy and understanding." The interest is not fulfilled for
two reasons: "first, that the narrative is entangled; secondly, that the entanglement is never given time to clear itself
while thought proceeds and action breathes more quickly.
The play is driven into the audience, on the principle of the
man who must always ride a bicycle at 20 miles an hour lest
he fall off, or of the conversationalist who dare not pause
for fear that another may capture the table." Crucial failure
to develop the character of Paul. "Paul is, or should have
been, the dramatist's means of discussing the theme of suffering and of purification by suffering. The drift, the anger,

the folly, the turbulence of the others would have had meaning if it had been related to him. As things are, he is
psychologically undiscovered until so late in the play that the
discovery itself seems arbitrary, and has no power to bind
the rest together. One early speech from him, steady and
coherent enough to show in which quarter his sun would
rise, might have given the whole play its bearings."

V.520. Ivor Brown, The Observer (August 14, 1938).
A "robust play of menace and panic, mercy and revenge,"
with "ideas above its station." Basil Dean tried "to make
melodrama wear the graces of High Art." "The action had
been intermittently exciting: the moral unquestionably up-
lifting: but the story was not only repetitive in the telling,
but uncommonly hard to swallow."

V.521. R.C., Sunday Times (August 14, 1938).
Play "hovers uneasily between discursiveness and crude
melodrama;" the "mixture of violence and polemics leaves no
room for the development of character." Neither the characters nor their world is believable.

V.522. New Statesman (August 20, 1938).
An ingenuous and arch play. "The ending is happy and the
moral excellent, but the Tolstoyan talk of love and Christ is
handled with embarrassing naivete." Play "is irritating, and
sometimes ridiculous, but it is not tedious."

V.523. Alan Bott, Tatler (August 24, 1938).
The ending is fine melodrama, but there is too much detail
in the early parts. The melodrama, the drama of human futility and the drama of redemption tend to cancel each other
out. "Mr Hutchinson is an unusually good novelist; but contrasts in manner, and evocative descriptions, from the past,
that usefully blend in a book of 100,000 words cannot be
compressed in 15,000 words of dialogue for living characters."

V.524. Weekly Review (August 25, 1938).
Argues that the play's politics are anti-Communist. Plenty
of Chekhovian interpolations, but Hutchinson's have no bear-
ing on the development of the characters, who are "puppets."
Badly directed so that all the actors are forced to shout.
Basil Dean created "a purposeless din." Thinks that Hutchinson's talent is unsuitable for the theatre. "His detail, as in
that fascinating study of sadism, Shining Scabbard, cannot
be translated into stage action, and the philosophic angle,
which in his novels he gets over so triumphantly, misses his
mark in the theatre."

V.525. C.M., New York Times (September 4, 1938).
Play "much more profound in thought than it appeared to be

on the stage. Not until the very end of the last act does
it become clear that this confusion is purposeful, that the
author is not a melodramatist, and that what he had in his
mind was that, among the turmoil of political hatreds, only
the principles of Christianity could prevail." Play would
have been improved had Paul's significance been established
earlier.

V.526.   Harold Hobson, Christian Science Monitor (September 20,
         1938).
         The biblical verse "is the basis of a last act that is profound-
         ly moving and deeply sincere, as well as dramatic in the high-
         est degree. The temper of the play as a whole may be too
         unrelievedly somber for many tastes, and it is written per-
         haps in too unvaried a key, but the climax, in which Zadol-
         ski and his companions are allowed to escape, is one of the
         finest things to be seen on the London stage. It is greatly
         to be regretted that it will soon be seen on the London stage
         no more. But it proves that in Mr R.C. Hutchinson, the
         author, whose celebrity as a novelist is already widespread,
         the theater has a recruit whose intensity of feeling, clarity
         of perception, and dramatic skill are qualities of the highest
         potential value."

V.527.   J.B. Priestley, New Statesman (September 25, 1943).
         In an article attacking the low standards of dramatic criti-
         cism, Priestley cites the reception of Hutchinson's play in
         1938, where a sensitive intelligent newcomer was mauled by
         hostile critics. "His play had its lapses, but they were the
         lapses of an intelligent creative mind not yet fully acquainted
         with all the demands and devices of the stage." The play
         should, instead, have been welcomed and then gently criti-
         cized.

W.   Memoir of R.C. Hutchinson

W.528.   The following delightful memoir of the novelist appears in
         the autobiography of Alec Waugh. Their meeting at the Test
         Match at Lord's Cricket Ground would have taken place in
         1946. Arthur Waugh had written a very interesting review
         of The Unforgotten Prisoner (see above, S.371) but it seems
         that Alec Waugh wrote nothing about Hutchinson apart from
         this tribute in The Best Wine Last:

                 That year an Indian Cricket XI was touring the
                 country. I had had a box at Lord's for the 1938
                 and 1939 Test Matches and my application this year
                 [1946] was accepted. The sun shone throughout the

match. I had brought back from New York a number of tins of chicken and salmon that were unobtainable in London then.

I brought up a crate of wine from Edrington. Wine was hard to get in London. My Beaujolais was as much appreciated as my sandwiches.

Among my guests that day was R.C. Hutchinson. In 1944 he had been sent out to Baghdad to write an official history of Paiforce. Until then I had scarcely known him. An acquaintance developed into a friendship. He was a delightful fellow, completely without conceit in spite of his high quality as a writer. His talk was that day one of the most pleasant features of the occasion. We had a lot to tell each other about our writing plans. "We must keep in touch with one another," we agreed. But we were never to meet again. It was very easy to lose touch in postwar England. Hutchinson was a recluse. I was away so much. We did not have any common ground. I think he was one of the most significant writers of our day.

He had a miraculous capacity to make real a place that he had never visited, as he showed in his picture of a French small town in Shining Scabbard and of Russia in Testament.

X. Miscellaneous Press Reports

This section, arranged in chronological order, includes reports of Hutchinson's sales, prizes, lectures, travels, etc., supplementing and confirming much of the material in the Biographical Notes section of this volume.

X.529. Career at Colman's
Reported that Hutchinson was Assistant to Mr. P.J. Mead, Advertising Manager of Colman's, Norwich. (Advertising World, March 1932)

X.530. THE ANSWERING GLORY
Hutchinson is quoted as saying that the novel's "theme is courage as humanity's highest common denominator. The suggestion being that courage takes its place beside love as part of the main strength of Christianity." (Sunday Chronicle, March 27, 1932).

X.531. ONE LIGHT BURNING
Reported that this is the week's best-selling novel in England.
(The Observer, February 17 & 24, 1935.)

X.532. THE ANSWERING GLORY
Reported that the novelist was a little bewildered at this novel's "being made a battleground by the Romanticists and Re-
alists," for he was by no means sure what these terms mean.
(Advertiser's Weekly, February 28, 1935.)

X.533. Contemporary Reputation
Reported that William Lyon Phelps praised Hutchinson and
James Hilton in a talk to the American Women's Club in Paris
(Daily Mail, Paris, May 25, 1935); and that in his annual
book lecture he had included One Light Burning among his
13 recommended novels (New York Herald Tribune, August
26, 1935).

X.534. SHINING SCABBARD
Reported that the novel was selling very well in England, behind Wodehouse's Laughing Gas and Mitchell's Gone With The
Wind (The Observer, October 4, 11 & 18, 1936); and that
in the US, it was one of the six best-selling novels, behind,
again, Gone With The Wind (New York Post, January 11,
1937); it was also reported that it sold 78,000 copies within
two weeks of publication in the United States (New York
Times, January 16, 1937). A year later it was reported that
the first edition of the novel, published in 1936 at 8/6d, was
worth 15/= in the trade (John O'London's Weekly, December
10, 1937).

X.535. Contemporary Reputation
"One of the foremost English literary magazines recently
named the novelists who really matter and 'have convincing
importance and significance.' Restricted to the authors of
England, the main selection was composed of Virginia Woolf,
Aldous Huxley, W.S. Maugham and H.G. Wells. A further
list is made up of those 'who have at least a hint of great-
ness in their work,' and consists of: Hugh Walpole, J.B.
Priestley, Frances Brett Young, Compton Mackenzie, David
Garnett, Wyndham Lewis, Richard Aldington, H.E. Bates,
R.C. Hutchinson, Ronald Fraser, E.M. Forster, and L.H.
Myers." (Sydney Morning Herald, November 30, 1937.)

X.536. Contemporary Reputation
Sir Hugh Walpole named Hutchinson as one of "the three
young novelists of whom one may expect ... fine things,"
the others being Greene and Isherwood. Hutchinson, Walpole remarked, "has not yet cleared his technical decks for
action, but these three men have all, in their different ways,
vitality, and are real creators with true creative zest."
(The Star, January 18, 1938.)

X.537. TESTAMENT
Reported that Hutchinson took over 2,000 hours to write the 300,000 words of this novel. (The Bookseller, July 21, 1938.)

X.538. Speech at Cheltenham
Report of the Meeting of the Cheltenham Literary Society at Queen's Hotel, October 20, 1938. Ernest Raymond warned of the dangers facing liberty of expression in England. Responding to the President's toast, Hutchinson deprecated the decline in the reading of serious literature, and said he believed that the plant of serious writing was worth cultivating. (Gloucester Echo, October 21, 1938; typescript of speech in MOHC.)

X.539. "Sunday Times" Gold Medal: TESTAMENT
Reported that Hutchinson had been awarded the "Sunday Times Gold Medal for Fiction" on November 14, 1938, Churchill winning the medal for biography with his Marlborough. The medal was received by Mrs. Margaret Hutchinson in her husband's absence. (The Times, November 15, 1938.)

X.540. Contemporary Reputation
Sir Hugh Walpole included Hutchinson among the day's leading novelists, alongside Wells, Maugham, Woolf, Forster, Huxley, Priestley, Bowen, Macauley, Swinnerton, L.A.G. Strong and Morgan. (Daily Sketch, December 28, 1938.)

X.541. P.E.N. Declaration Against Nazis
Hutchinson was one of the members of the International P.E.N. Club to sign a declaration appealing for the support of the rest of the world in Britain's fight against Nazi power. Other signatories included Wells, Forster and Rebecca West. (The Bookseller, June 20, 1940.)

X.542. THE FIRE AND THE WOOD
Reported that the novel was, respectively, ninth and tenth on the US best-seller lists. (New York Herald Tribune, October 20 & 27, 1940.)

X.543. Home Guard Speech
Reported that Hutchinson wrote the speech delivered by King George VI at the Stand-Down Parade of the Home Guard in Hyde Park on December 3, 1944. (The Times, December 4, 1944.)

X.544. Letter About "Paiforce."
Hutchinson wrote a letter to the Editor of The Times about "Paiforce":

In The Times of March 6 a Correspondent lately in

Persia, referring to the supply of war material to
Russia by the southern route, writes: "While the
running of the railway from the Persian Gulf to Tehe-
ran was soon handed over to the Americans, British
troops remained responsible for the security both of
the railway and of the roads...." This sentence
may, I think, have the unintended effect of belit-
tling an epic achievement of the British Army.

In October 1941, when Brigadier Sir Godfrey Rhodes
and his staff began to re-organize and develop the
Trans-Iranian Railway, it could carry only 200 tons
of paying loads a day. In almost every department
the organization of the line was, by occidental standards, chaotic. Half the locomotives were awaiting
repair and the rest in a parlous condition. The
Royal Engineers, exercising extraordinary tact and
patience, had to overhaul the Gilbertian edifice from
top to bottom, to carry out a huge constructional
programme, and to keep the line in operation at the
same time. Working double-headed trains through
the 140 tunnels (some spiral) between Andimeshk
and Dorud, British locomotive crews were often overcome by the fumes and the terrible heat. Some Sap-
pers died; but the loads which the Russians so desperately needed always got through. By the end of
1942 the monthly lift had been multiplied nearly
eight times.

The Americans, coming with comparatively unlimited
resources, were able greatly to increase the lift
again. They richly deserved the tributes widely
paid to their achievement. But in justice to the
British engineers it should be remembered that the
Americans took over a system already completely re-
organized and enormously developed by British stam-
ina and skill.

The British remained responsible for inland water
transport and continued to run convoys over the
formidable western section of the 3,000-mile road
system put in order by Persian contractors under
R.E. supervision. The contribution of Paiforce
(Persia and Iraq Command) to the "Aid to Russia"
lift was never limited to protective duties. The
whole story had to be kept dark for reasons of security, and in consequence a splendid achievement
by thousands of British and Indian soldiers in the
conquest of distance and climate has received piti-
fully small recognition.

Yours faithfully,
R.C. Hutchinson.
Garrick Club, W.C.2. (The Times, March 19, 1946.)

X.545.   PAIFORCE
Question asked in the House of Commons by George Jeger,
M.P., about the delay in the appearance of Paiforce. Mr.
Shinwell, Secretary of State for War, replied that the "pro-
duction of this book has been delayed by work of more ur-
gent public importance. The text is in proof, and work upon
the illustrations and maps should be completed by the end of
March. This should allow the book to be published during
the summer." (Undated clipping from Hansard, presumably
January/February 1948.)

X.546.   Visit to New York: ELEPHANT AND CASTLE
Announcement of Hutchinson's arrival in New York on September 18, 1948, "for his first visit to the United States" to
publicize the forthcoming Elephant and Castle which appeared
from Rinehart's in January 1949 (New York Times, September
16, 1948); it was later reported that after Hutchinson's return to England, Rinehart's cabled him, asking what present
he would like to mark the novel's US publication. It was reported that he had asked for "a gallon of chocolate ice-
cream" and that this was shipped from La Guardia on a Pan
American flight on January 27, 1949 (New York Herald Tribune, January 28, 1949). [In conversation, Mrs. Hutchinson
has denied that her husband had requested what was, at
that time, such a luxurious gift.]

X.547.   Interview in New York
Report of Hutchinson's interview with Harry Hansen. He
said that his principal literary admirations were Tolstoy,
Thackeray and, among contemporaries, Elizabeth Bowen. He
said that he was keen to begin reading Willa Cather. (Chicago Tribune, October 17, 1948.)

X.548.   Talk
Reported that Hutchinson gave a talk, entitled "A Flight to
America," to the Farnham, Surrey, Women's Institute.
(Farnham Herald, February 4, 1949.)

X.549.   ELEPHANT AND CASTLE
Reported that the first printing of the novel was 25,000
copies, with the US Book-of-the-Month Club guaranteeing a
further 170,000 (Chicago Tribune, February 6, 1949). It
was later reported that the novel was eighth on the US best-
seller list, behind Douglas' The Big Fisherman and Mailer's
The Naked and The Dead (New York Times, March 13, 1949);
and later that it was thirteenth, behind Bowen's Heat of the
Day and Paton's Cry The Beloved Country (New York Herald

Tribune, April 3, 1949). In Britain it was reported to be a best-seller alongside Mann's *Dr. Faustus* (*The Recorder*, May 21, 1949).

X.550. Chairs Templars Meeting
Reported that Hutchinson took the chair of a meeting at Hindhead, Surrey, on June 21, 1950, when L.A.G. Strong talked on "Contemporary English Writing" at a Conference School for the Grand Lodge of Sweden, International Order of Good Templars. (*Farnham Herald*, June 23, 1950.)

X.551. THE STEPMOTHER
This novel was discussed by Arthur Calder-Marshall in "Talking of Books," BBC Home Service, October 23, 1955.

X.552. Letter on Copyright
Hutchinson was one of eight signatories to a letter from "The Society of Authors" on the proposed Copyright Bill, the others including Graham Greene and Rebecca West. The letter was an attempt to protect writers' "ancillary rights" in film and in periodicals. (*The Times*, November 4, 1955.)

X.553. MARCH THE NINTH
Reported that Twentieth Century-Fox had purchased the film rights of *March The Ninth* in advance of publication. (*Variety*, New York, October 16, 1957.)

X.554. BBC Talk
Hutchinson was one of six speakers who recalled one of the year's books that was of particular interest in "The World of Books," BBC Network Three, December 21, 1957.

X.555. MARCH THE NINTH
Hutchinson reported on the origin of this novel: "A year's work on a novel [presumably this is the "unfinished novel" about which Hutchinson spoke on the BBC in October 1956], exploring, from a standpoint of Christian philosophy, the character of a woman responsible for gross atrocities in a concentration camp, went into the wastepaper basket and I turned to an entirely different theme and wrote *The Stepmother*. But the problem which the discarded novel tried to solve remained in my mind, as did my impressions of the ordinary men and women accused at the International Military Tribunal at Nuremberg." (*The Bookman*, November 1957.)

X.556. Visit to Belfast
Reported that Hutchinson visited the Belfast Branch of the Irish P.E.N. in May 1959, his first visit to Ulster in forty years. (*Belfast Telegraph*, January 19 & May 23, 1959.)

X.557. THE STEPMOTHER

Reported that Neil Paterson had finished writing the script of The Stepmother for filming by Paramount. (Scottish Daily Express, April 15, 1961.)

X.558. RSL Fellowship
Report that Hutchinson had been elected a Fellow of the Royal Society of Literature on June 7, 1962, the other election being that of Christopher Hibbert. (Yorkshire Post, June 8, 1962.)

X.559. Letter on University Libraries
Hutchinson wrote a letter to The Times on the subject of university libraries. (The Times, August 16, 1963.)

X.560. A CHILD POSSESSED
Canon K.R. Prebble, Vicar of St. Paul's, Auckland, and author of the entry on Hutchinson in Contemporary Novelists, preached a sermon based on the novel in St. Mary's Cathedral, Auckland, on July 11, 1965. (St. Paul's Parish News, August 1965.)

X.561. Speech to English Association
Hutchinson spoke at the annual meeting of the English Association on the novelist's struggle with language, June 26, 1965. (Manuscript of speech, 5 pages fcap, in MOHC.)

X.562. W.H. Smith Award: A CHILD POSSESSED
Hutchinson wrote a letter (draft in MOHC) to Mr. Michael Hornby, W.H. Smith Ltd., dated July 22, 1966, expressing "delight" and "gratitude" at the award. "The news immeasurably strengthens my morale at a time when that recruitment is much needed." In a later letter (draft in MOHC) to Mr. S.T. Hyde, Managing Director of W.H. Smith Advertising Ltd., August 28, 1966, he thanked Mr. Hyde for their lunch on August 25, and inquired about the wording of the invitation to the award ceremony, being apprehensive that an author receiving such an invitation might believe that he was the prize's recipient and "then his disappointment would be unbearably painful." In a further letter to Mr. Hyde (draft in MOHC), September 3, 1966, he sends a list of guests to be invited to the ceremony at the Savoy Hotel: Richard Church, Mr. and Mrs. Graeme Hendrey (Eiluned Lewis, the novelist), Col. and Mrs. Jocelyn Gibb, Mr. and Mrs. Spencer Curtis Brown, Professor and Mrs. Guy Chapman (Storm Jameson, the novelist), Mr. and Mrs. Ernest Raymond, Pamela Frankau, Mr. and Mrs. Eric Gillett, The Lord Horder (of Gerald Duckworth Ltd.), Sir George and Lady Rostrevor Hamilton, Mr. and Mrs. Robert Gittings, Mr. and Mrs. Harold Hobson, Mr. and Mrs. Maurice Denham, Anthony Marlowe, Mr. and Mrs. Sean Day-Lewis, Mr. and Mrs. Cyril Luckham, Mr. and Mrs. R.E. Keen (BBC), Mr.

and Mrs. Kennison Preston. At the prize-giving ceremony
on November 9, 1966, Hutchinson was reported to have said:
"I believe there will be more joy in Barclay's Bank, Cater-
ham, over this one cheque than over ninety and nine accounts which need no adjustment." He also said: "My own
view is that the novel only comes to its full stature when it
defies every determinist philosophy, when it accepts the mysterious, the numinous, when it recognizes in every human
being not only a marvellous machinery but also a unique and
divine creation."

The prize of Ł1,000 was presented by Jennie Lee, Minister
for the Arts, and the Judges were Lady Huntingdon, Rupert
Hart-Davis and Raymond Mortimer. (London Life, October
12, 1966.) Hutchinson was reported as saying that A Child
Possessed "is not by any means my best, but it is one that
I am particularly fond of." He indicated that the story had
been suggested by his visit to some mongol children, "some
of them were hideous, but all of them had the most beautiful
smiles--they were complete and lovable human beings. It
was that revelation which inspired the book." (Evening
Standard, November 9, 1966.)

Sir Rupert Hart-Davis is reported to have said of the novel:
"I would be surprised if anyone finished this novel without
feeling purged of fear and pity." (Yorkshire Post, November 10, 1966.)

Storm Jameson commented that "of the thirteen novels ... at
least six are major works. His new novel adds a seventh
to a series of books which entitle him to be considered as
the finest living novelist, the only one who cannot be judged
without evoking the names of the great European novelists."
(The Bookseller, November 12, 1966.)

X.563. BBC Interview
Hutchinson interviewed on Woman's Hour by Marjorie Ander-
son, February 8, 1967.

X.564. Pamela Frankau
Hutchinson wrote to Dame Rebecca West (draft in MOHC),
June 1967, thanking her for the obituary she wrote for The
Times on the occasion of Miss Frankau's death.

X.565. Letter to "The Times" on "Shortened Bible"
Hutchinson wrote to The Times on this subject. (The Times,
December 10, 1969.)

X.566. ORIGINS OF CATHLEEN
Agatha Christie reported as saying that Hutchinson was a
"favourite author" and that Origins of Cathleen was "inter-

esting and amusing and sometimes very tragic." (<u>Oxford Mail</u>, November 23, 1972.)

X.567. Booker Prize: <u>RISING</u>
Before the Booker shortlist had been announced, Ladbroke's, the London bookmakers, announced the odds on the twelve "most highly-fancied runners," David Storey's <u>Saville</u>, the eventual winner, being favorite at 3-1 with the posthumously published <u>Rising</u> at 12-1. (<u>Sunday Times</u>, October 31, 1976.) <u>Rising</u> was indeed short-listed for the Ł5,000 prize and was then quoted at 4-1. It was reported that it "followed a journey to South America by cargo boat in 1971." The judges were Walter Allen, Francis King and Lady Mary Wilson. (<u>Yorkshire Post</u>, November 4, 1976.)

APPENDIX: HUTCHINSON'S CRITICAL ESSAYS

Unlike many English novelists in the twentieth century, Hutchinson, at no stage of his career, supplemented his income by reviewing in the literary weeklies or the "quality" press. About his own work, too, he wrote only sparingly, and he gave few interviews to journalists. The three most important critical essays among such a small crop were published between 1949 and 1953, at the height of his commercial success (see above, Q.331), and are reprinted below, since they are difficult to obtain outside of specialist, academic libraries, and have never been reprinted.

The first, "My Apologia," appeared in John O'London's Weekly on April 15, 1949, three days after the publication in London of Elephant and Castle, and was also published, as "If One Must Write Fiction...," in The Saturday Review of Literature, September 3, 1949. "My First Novel" was published in The Listener on April 2, 1953, at a time when Hutchinson was writing The Stepmother or, possibly, the unfinished novel about Nazi atrocities (X.555, above). The last piece, "The Pace for Living," was also published in The Listener, on September 17 of the same year.

Y.568. "My Apologia"

The desire to write novels sometimes seems to me a kind of disease. It afflicts many people, either early or late in life, but the majority make a good recovery. I have been less fortunate.

It first attacked me when the works of Amy Le Feuvre were being read to me in the nursery, and during my second year at boarding school I produced a novel of 20,000 words; its nature and literary merit are sufficiently indicated by the title--The Hand of the Purple Idol. This eruption might have cured me, but it failed to do so; as soon as I had left Oxford and gone into business I was at work on another, which unfortunately found a publisher, and I continued, while I worked as assistant to the advertising manager for Colman's Mustard, to spend nearly all my spare time writing. In the next few years I produced The Answering Glory, a portrait of a woman missionary which I still like, The Unforgotten Prisoner, a crudely shaped story set in the early post-first-war years in Germany and England--the Book Society gave me some much-needed encouragement by choosing it--One Light Burning, a tale of Siberian adventure which had a modest succès d'estime in some quarters, and the earlier chapters of Shining Scabbard, set in the provincial France of 1914.

To do one job by day and another at night made a fairly hard life; but if, when young, one must write, I think one can do worse than follow that course. The period when one is learning the elements of a writer's job by trial and error is necessarily a long one, and since it is unlikely that the public will want to buy in quantity the products of that apprenticeship it seems to me better to have the security of steady employment than to be burdened with anxiety about selling what one writes.

To this reasoning, however, experience brought objections. The mind may be most creative at night, when fatigue makes competing interests less aggressive; but it is, I find, most critical in the morning, and only a fresh mind can perform the task--so much harder for a writer than for a painter-- of standing back to view the picture (a section or a chapter) as a whole. A paragraph which seems to read well enough in the small hours may reveal itself in daylight as loose-jointed, tortuous, over-rhythmic or ill-proportioned....

My dissatisfactions were increasing. I was beginning (far later I suppose than most writers) to realize that the technical problems were not the only ones; that a novel, to be worth the effort that goes to its making, ought ideally to perform a larger operation on the reader's mind than distracting it for two or three hours; in short, that I had everything still to learn, and that I should make no progress unless I made writing a wholetime job. This was in 1935, and I then had three children. To give up my regular employment called for a recklessness of which I should have been quite incapable; but my wife (who has always been my chief literary adviser) possessed the nerve I lacked, we moved our family to a converted public-house in the Cotswolds and I "commenced author."

Keeping to a fixed schedule of working hours (for if I worked only when inclined I should scarcely work at all), I finished Shining Scabbard in what now seems to me a remarkably short time. This was probably the tidiest novel I have done --it has, I think, fewer technical blunders than the others-- but was fatally lacking in philosophical implications of any kind: it poses no problem concerned with the opposition of good and evil. It was the choice of the Book of the Month

Club in America. This was a long book, but the next one, Testament, a story set in the Russia of 1916-1920, was longer still--perhaps 300,000 words. Great length may indicate pretentiousness, or laziness of a particular kind, and my own general feeling is that a contemporary novel gains in many ways if it can be kept within 100,000 words. I cannot give shortly all the reasons why I have considerably exceeded that figure four times; I can only say that the portion of life I wanted to represent on each of those four occasions could not, in my judgment, be represented in a small space with fidelity.

The situations and events of a novel can derive importance only from the importance of the people who take part in them, which may mean, in broad terms, that the reader must know those people as he knows his own friends. In life such intimate knowledge is acquired as a rule slowly, and in fiction I doubt if any knowledge which is emptied, so to speak, into the reader's plate will affect him as profoundly as that which is administered in scientific doses. Indeed, I suspect that slowness (the tedium of which ought to be cunningly alleviated) is an element essential to the novelistic form--as opposed to the dramatic or short-story form. Incidentally, it is not true in my experience that a long novel is easier to write than a short one; length obviates a number of tactical problems, but it induces strategic ones--problems of proportion and momentum--which are by no means easier to handle.

I have been asked more than once how the knowledge of Russia needed for the background of Testament was obtained. The answer is grievously simple. Municipal libraries contain many books by amateur travellers, naive autobiographers, excitable diarists and others, which are full of odd bits of information, available to anyone who will take the trouble to hunt them out. Background material is the least formidable of a novelist's difficulties; it involves donkey work, nothing more.

I had determined to write one novel which would satisfy me as a good one before I passed the age of thirty. But in 1938, when I finished Testament, I was already thirty-one, so I put the age limit on to forty. With the optimism that comes from an Irish strain I imagined that another nine years would suffice.

The business was growing more difficult. Belatedly, I was coming to see that the aims of the novelist and those of an artist (of however modest ambition) were at least superficially opposed. The desire--the passion--of a novelist is to represent the fullness of life, and life is an untidy affair--

a procession of infinitely varied relationships, of boredom, triviality, melodrama and farce, of incidents which differ totally in colour and shape according to the point from which they are viewed.

The essence of a work of art is unity. If a novelist has, besides the instinct of a story-teller, that aesthetic instinct which one associates more immediately with painters and composers, he hankers to impose on every part of his book-- description, narrative, dialogue--a tonal unity of the kind which a painter achieves by the selection and modification of colours, and which Beethoven imposes by analogous means upon a symphony. The ambition may be futile. Certainly I find, in a way not easy to set down in terms, that whenever I am writing, the aesthetic and what I may call the historian's instincts are at war; and in the work of others it often appears to me that the writing which I most admire aesthetically has been achieved at the expense of certain robust virtues on which the final importance of the novel seems to depend.

At the age of thirty-two, however, one still considers no problem insuperable, and in this light I was contentedly overhauling my previous notions of storytelling when the signature of the Munich agreement indicated that artistic ambitions must shortly be put into store. I had finished another book in a scramble (The Fire and the Wood, a story concerned with tuberculosis, destined to come out at the wrong time and to be a failure) when I went into the Army early in 1940.

The Army treated me with exceptional charity. It presented me with some of the best friends I have known, a great variety of employment, and a journey through Egypt, Palestine, Syria, Iraq and Persia which I could never have afforded as a civilian: it even gave me the opportunity, during a tour at the War Office, to write one short novel, Interim-- working late at night, as in earlier days, with the additional incubus of A.A. guns shaking my tiny top-floor Kensington room. Soldiering, if my activities could be dignified by that name, was a healthy change of occupation and no one who, physically fit in 1939, found himself in the same physical condition at the end of 1945 has the smallest excuse for grumbling about his lot. I only mention, as a fact, that the gap of five and a half years in the very middle of my professional life was no more helpful to me than to people in other callings.

Perhaps unfortunately, it left my appetite for writing fiction unabated. Very soon after demobilization I was at work on a London novel, Elephant and Castle, which I had planned

before the war. The disease, in fact, still had its hold on
a patient who had not the smallest wish to be cured. I
found that after the long interval it was necessary to start
learning again, more painfully, much that I thought I had
learnt before about the business of constructing a novel, of
using words, which are intractable material, to convey to
"the reader" (mysterious, tetchy, hostile creature) the ex-
citements which one's people and events have provoked in
oneself. The task does not grow less laborious, the problems are never solved. It continues to be a whole-time job
(which I vary with amateurish attention to Church work and
to an entrancing family) and I mean to pursue this occupation as long as the state of the world, the tolerance of my
bankers and my own mental physique allow.

The intention is hard to rationalize or justify. Of the several occupations I have tried, this one is very much the
hardest, the loneliest, the most continuously exasperating.
I frequently think that it is also the most selfish. The
priest and the ploughman are necessary to mankind. Those
who make soap or sell bicycles perform services which justify their existence. Even the story-teller, if he sticks to
romance or detection, fulfils a need of human society. But
it is not evident that the novelist who spends all his time
trying to satisfy what he calls his artistic conscience is ful-
filling any such need. Further, I fancy that if such a novelist tries to ease his moral conscience by deliberately introducing a didactic element into his work he generally
courts disaster: the control which he exercises upon his
characters derives from certain intuitions, and if, forsaking
those intuitions, he uses characters as instruments for teaching moral lessons, they will die. Moral passion, taken at
boiling point, may produce work which has both moral and
artistic value. Fiction derived from a calculated morality
will have neither.

That statement, however, I believe to be incomplete. The
novelist portrays people--their behaviour, thoughts, emo-
tions--but such portrayal will not result in a novel until it
has been shaped by artistic process. Art implies pattern;
in the novel, a pattern of human relationships, which is inevitably a moral pattern; and in practice the intuitions by
which the actions of a novel are controlled are at least partly of a moral nature. The opposition between artistic and
moral purposes proves, in the end, to be only a superficial
one. The fundamental concern of the fictionist is to represent truth as he perceives it, with the greatest possible fidelity; on that fidelity the artistic value of his work depends,
and it would at least be difficult to argue that this concern
has no relation to morality. Shortly, I believe that in so far
as he succeeds in the artistic purpose of illuminating an area

of truth--the actualities of human nature--the novelist per-
forms a unique function which cannot be without moral value.

To explore the implications of this view would need a paper
several times as long as this. Here, without wishing to be
dogmatic (since dogmatism is not the prerogative of authors),
I can only suggest that a certain absence of stature which
has been observed in much contemporary fiction may be due
to the mechanistic conception of human character which now
widely prevails; for if the human being is considered merely as the resultant of heredity, environment, definable com-
plexes, then the description of his mental and physical behaviour comes to have only the interest which attaches to
problems in mathematics. The splendour possible in fiction
will never come, I think, except from discovering in every
human (good or bad, intelligent or idiotic) a value far higher
than that which he derives from having, in the last few hundred millennia, come to surpass the lower animals in sen-
tience and understanding: an individual and unique value,
acquired from an extra-natural source.

I fancy that the raison d'être of a novelist is to be found in
that conception, which is fundamental to his business; and
also, as I understand it, fundamental in the Christian philosophy.

Y.569. "My First Novel"

Not long ago I was poking about in a secondhand bookshop
in Lincoln, and I was suddenly confronted by a copy of a
novel with the awkward title Thou Hast A Devil. It was my
first published book. The cover was mildewed, but it had
not suffered from any hard usage, so I bought it--it cost
me 4d--meaning to put it in the first convenient stove. On
the way home, in the train, I opened it and read a few para-
graphs. And I said to myself: 'Is this excruciating work
a faithful portrait of my own mind when I was twenty-one?'

When I tried to get back inside that adolescent mind--to
think and feel exactly as I had thought and felt twenty-five
years before--I found that it could not be done. I remembered, of course, the circumstances in which the book was
written. They were not romantic. I was not starving in a
garret, and I did not write on the backs of menus or race-
cards. I was living by myself in a flat--or what counted
for a flat--in the city of Norwich in 1929, and during the
day I was employed by a firm of manufacturers in covering
very large sheets of paper with very tiny figures--for what
purpose I never exactly discovered. This was an especially

cold winter; and on days when there was thick snow on the
ground, the old lady who was supposed to come in and 'do'
for me did not arrive; so I used to get home in the evenings
to find my bed unmade and my greasy breakfast things still
on the table. Before that situation could be dealt with, the
waste pipe of the sink had to be unfrozen with kettles of
boiling water. It was only when all this sordid housewifery
had been disposed of--that is to say, about eight or nine
o'clock--that I could get down to my 'masterpiece,' and I
wrote something like 1,000 words a night. That rather stag-
gers me: I could not go at such a pace now. But then, in
most ways, one's first book is much the easiest to write.
You see, until you have been chased around a little by reviewers and people you are full of confidence. You are quite
un-self-critical. Any joke you manufacture seems to you
vastly amusing, your dialogue sounds commendably similar
to the dialogue you have read in other people's books, your
descriptive passages appear to you shrewdly turned and
rather harmonious. All I worried about--as far as I can re-
member--was whether the thing would go to 80,000 words.
I had been told that 80,000 was the minimum length a publisher would look at, and it seemed to me a depressingly
long haul.

I must have been aware that there was such a thing as lit-
erature--after all I had been through my Gosse and my
Saintsbury at school. But with all my vanity, I never imagined that literature was something I might try to emulate.
All I wanted was to produce a book--which meant 80,000
words. No, wait! It is not true to say that I only hoped
to produce a book. What I wanted, and I am confessing to
a degree of fatuity which now appals me, was to turn out a
'brilliant' book.

I had what I believed, in my innocence, to be an entirely
new theme, a rendering of the New Testament story in a
modern setting, or rather, what was supposed to be the near
future, with people going about in enormous airships. This
theme (about which I was entirely, and properly, serious)
was going, I thought, to create a considerable stir, and I
foresaw that my whole life would be altered when it was published. I imagined that editors who had previously returned
my short stories with unfailing regularity would soon be
eager to accept them. I saw myself quite shortly bidding a
crisp farewell to my employers, and becoming what I had
dreamed of being from my early childhood--a professional
writer. Or did I soberly believe in all that fantasy? I do
not really know.

It was thanks to the kindness of Philip Gibbs, who gave me
a personal introduction to his literary agent, that this pre-

posterous work did, after many days and many journeys, get published. It earned me £27. It was reviewed--with touching forbearance--in, I think, one London and one provincial paper. And I suppose one or two generous people may even have bought it: some optimist must have bought the copy which I found in Lincoln. Anyway, that was the end of the incident, except that it failed to cure me of wanting to write.

Yes, that first effort of mine was an imperial hash. But when I say that I wish I had never written the wretched thing, am I being perfectly sincere? I am not certain that it was a total waste of time. To start with, it seems to be a necessity for novelists to get certain things out of their systems. For example, many of us find it therapeutically necessary at one time or another to write a novel with a London setting. I myself often have the foolish notion that I shall not die happy unless I have delivered myself of an appallingly long epic about life in the interior of China. One might go as far as to say that a novelist's life consists of nothing else but getting things out of his system. You remember the professional writer in Chekhov's play, 'The Seagull,' the one who says: 'Here I see a cloud that looks like a grand piano. I think that I must put into a story, somewhere, that a cloud sailed by that looked like a grand piano.' That is only just a caricature of the novelist's mentality.

That first book probably got something out of my system-- something that was spurious, some naive romanticism, certain facile judgments, a good deal of adolescent froth. But the fact that it went into print may have done more for me than that. I cannot say how soon I realised that I had produced a wad of balderdash. But I do know that to see in print something you have written yourself is nearly always a salutary punishment. Any piece of work is altered in colour, in feeling, at every stage of its journey from the brain to the printed page. To start with, the idea that is in your mind-- when you are shaving, or raking out the kitchen boiler--becomes different when it has been hammered into words. But as long as it is in your own handwriting, studded with your own corrections, it remains private. When it is turned into typescript, and then into galley-proofs, the work gets further away from you. And when those proofs are cut up into pages, you are able to see the product of your mind almost as if it were not your own at all.

I do not say you can get completely detached from it. It may take you some years to do that. But the thing does become sufficiently foreign to let you make something like an objective judgment. And in that way my first book may have started teaching me the writer's job. It is a job, you see, which no one else can teach you. At least, no one can teach you much. Of course there are writers who appear to enter the field already fully equipped. They know precisely what they want to communicate, what climate they want to create in the reader's mind, what tools they have at their disposal. I was not like that, and I do not believe I should have got like that by sitting at the feet of, say, Henry James. I had to discover for myself what are the problems of technique. By which I mean--very broadly--the problem of putting ideas which interest you into the reader's mind and at the same time preventing him from falling asleep (of course one always hopes that this reader is suffering from chronic insomnia, but one cannot rely on that). To begin with, I had no idea that such a difficulty existed. I went at the job bald-headed, because I did not realize then that any special equipment was necessary. If I had not started that way I should never have started at all. And if the thing had not found a publisher I might well have given up the dream of making writing my profession. Which, from my own point of view, would have been a pity.

Voltaire, I think it was, said that if he had a son who wanted to write, he would strangle him out of sheer loving kindness. I recognise the wisdom of that remark. Of the ways of making a living which I have tried, writing is very much the hardest, as well as the loneliest. There must be few occupations quite so rich in disappointments. But, if you have the novelist's bacillus inside you, you will never be really contented, I think, in any other trade.

The really shocking thing about my first book was that it was 'manufactured.' It contained an idea which was genuine--something I felt about intensely--but instead of letting that idea grow into a book I built a ramshackle edifice with just one room to house it. Nothing resembling a work of art can be produced like that. And yet I do believe, now, that the impulse which made me set to work and churn out those 80,000 words was not merely a puerile wish to startle and impress my friends. Something else, I think, was at work, something I can only explain like this: Suppose you are in Paris, travelling on the Metro. Standing near you there is a very old and very dirty woman, wearing those unbelievably thick, black stockings which are almost the uniform of her kind. Beside her there is a tiny, white-faced boy with spindle legs and a dribbly nose. The train lurches violently, and the old woman puts her hand on the boy's shoulder to steady him. He looks up at her, perhaps with a slight impatience, because he thinks he is too old for that sort of mothering. She looks down at him, and smiles faintly. Then he smiles back. You know, at once, that he is her grandson--possibly her only grandchild. You know, at the same moment, that all her love, all her pride, are centred in him. But much more than that. In the instant when those two people exchange smiles you see represented a huge tract of human experience--you feel, all at once, that in the excitement and the beauty of that exchange, everything in earth and Heaven has been revealed to you.

That is a common experience; I suppose nearly everyone has had something like it. And most people--being sensible-- are content to preserve it as a memory. But there is a kind of person so afflicted, mentally, that he cannot be happy until he has tried to get the experience into a form in which it can be imparted to someone else. The whole of it, I mean. Not just the incident, but the significance of it--the entire world of relationships and feelings which the incident has called into the light. And this kind of person is compelled to make that attempt, even if it costs him five years' hard labour and half a million words.

Again and again, he will be defeated. Words are a recalcitrant metal to work in--they resist you, the patterns they fall into are stale patterns, they obliterate subtleties, they can kill the ideas you mean them to illuminate. But the beginner does not realize that--he, in his simplicity, thinks that language is a treasury made for his particular use. And the man who has the writer's disease will never accept the truth that the possibilities of language are limited. He knows well enough that book after book has failed to convey the magic of life as he has seen it. But he still believes that in the next one--or the one after that--he will capture that mystery, he will achieve the impossible, he will produce something which perfectly satisfies himself. Then, he thinks, the disgrace of all the early fumblings will be wiped out.

Y.570.   "The Pace for Living"

I saw a play in Dublin not long ago in which the chief character was an elderly corn-merchant in a small Irish country town. He was a man of many anxieties--his heart was dicky, his nephew was cheating him, his wife had had the fantastic notion of spending ₤10 on a holiday. Altogether the pace of life was getting too much for him, and in a moment of despair he uttered a great cry from the heart: 'They tell me there's an aeroplane now that goes at 1,000 miles an hour. Now that's <u>too fast</u>!'

For me that was the most enchanting line in the play--the man's complaint was so gloriously irrelevant to his own situation. And besides being comic, it struck me as a perfect illustration of the way the Irish get at subtle truths by the most unlikely approaches. You saw what the old fool meant.

Not that I have any dislike of rapid movement myself. I enjoy going in a car at ninety miles an hour--so long as I am driving and so long as it is not my car. I adore the machines that hurl you about at Battersea. To dine in London and lunch in New York next day seems to me a most satisfactory experience: I admit it excludes all the real pleasures of travel--the sort of fun you get from a country bus in Somerset or Spain--but it gives you a superficial sense of drama; it was a sort of excitement our ancestors had to do without, and we might just as well accept it gratefully. No, where speed becomes something unfriendly to me is where the mental activities of our time tend--as they naturally do-- to follow the pace of the machines.

I speak with prejudice because I belong to the tribe of slow thinkers, those who are cursed with l'esprit de l'escalier: people who light on the most devastating repartee about four hours after the party's over. I am one of those who are guaranteed to get the lowest marks in any intelligence test, because these tests--or all the ones I have come across-- seem to be designed to measure the speed of your mind more than anything else. Obviously we slow thinkers are terribly handicapped in the business of getting a living, because if you cannot keep up with the machines, or the men behind the machines, you are not worth employing. But what I am thinking about just now is not so much the practical use of one's mind as its use for enjoyment.

As an example, when I go to the cinema I find myself in a hopeless fog, and after two or three minutes I have to turn to my wife for enlightenment. I whisper: 'Is this the same girl as the one we saw at the beginning?' And she whispers back: 'No, there are three girls in this film--a tall blonde, a short blonde, and a medium-sized brunette. Call them A, B, and C. The hero is that man who takes his hat off when he comes indoors. He is going to fall in love with girls B, C, and A, in that order.' And so it proves to be. There you have a mind which has trained itself to work in high gear--though as a matter of fact it can work in other gears just as well. But my point is that most of my fellow-patients in the cinema do think fast enough to keep up comfortably with rapid changes of scene and action. They think much faster than people did thirty years ago: possibly because those who do not think fast in the High Street nowadays may not get another chance in this world to think at all.

You can see that this rapidity which the cinema gives its audiences, and demands from them, must have its effect on other sorts of entertainment as well. Some time before the war I was talking to a famous theatrical producer about play construction; and he said something like this: 'The cinema has taught people the trick of early anticipation, and they bring their cinema minds into the theatre. This means that the playwright has to be five times as nimble as he was a few years ago if he wants to keep one jump ahead of his audience.' I imagine that today anyone with a long experience in the theatre would say the same thing with even greater emphasis.

And surely it would be surprising if people who have grown accustomed to a much faster movement in films and plays were content with written fiction which went at the old speeds. Of course they are not. Editors, who presumably know what their customers want, are demanding shorter and shorter stories with faster and faster action--stories which go off the mark like Olympic sprinters and keep up the pace right through to the tape. In America, where they carry these things to a logical conclusion, they have developed a technique for teaching people to read more quickly, and at the same time they have introduced devices for giving them less to read. They have literary surgeons over there who can take a novel of well over 400 pages, and, with a skill that really is astonishing, they can strip it right down to forty pages--using the author's own sentences, or parts of them, giving you most of the plot and nearly all the characters; and even a dash or two of the original scenery. Before long they may be able to turn out a pre-digested version of Dante's Divina Commedia which the tired business man can assimilate in fifteen minutes by stop-watch.

I confess I do not like this. I have a professional interest in fiction--I am a producer of that class of merchandise-- and I believe that the novel, as distinct from the short story or novelette, is meant to be a slow form of art. It would be presumptuous for an author to dogmatize about what the novelist's business is: that can be left to the younger critics. But it is fairly safe to say that one of the most interesting things (I avoid the word 'important') that novelists have done in the past is the creation of characters so immense in stature and significance that they have become part of the civilised world's inheritance; and as a rule these tremendous figures of fiction have been created by a slow process. The writers have asked for a large amount of the reader's time, sometimes a good deal of his patience; and, by using a very great number of small, skilful strokes, they have gradually, slowly, brought the whole man to life.

As I see it, the stature and slowness go together. It can be argued that Tolstoy, for example, was a wickedly discursive writer, that he was guilty of all sorts of irrelevance. But I wonder if Anna Karenina would be what she is to us--at one a woman of colossal tragic stature and an intimate acquaintance--if Tolstoy had squeezed her portrait into the length of The Vicar of Wakefield. Again, could Don Quixote, the romantic half-wit, have become a person who seems in some way to represent the aspirations and the weakness of all humanity, if Cervantes had confined his adventures so that they could be read in a couple of hours? It is said very often that the writers of our own day are incapable of creating important characters. That may be true. But if they were to ask for the patience which their predecessors confidently expected, would they get it, from readers who are used to the accelerated action of the films, people who have to do all their reading between Woking and Waterloo stations, because travel has become so rapid and convenient that there is no time to read in a chair at home?

I can see that on the face of it my objection is rather ridiculous. I seem to be saying, in effect, that there is something wrong about the 'tempo' of our own day because it does not suit the convenience of one or two old-fashioned literary types who hanker after a particular kind of writing. Of course, the complaint is not worth a moment's attention--unless the sort of writing I have mentioned does in fact correspond with something permanent in human experience; unless the slownesses in life itself which such writing reflects are something of unalterable value.

But I believe there are such slownesses. The rhythms of nature remain unchanged, and in that sense the tempo at which we live is not affected by the tempo at which we tear about. To live to the age of seventy takes seventy years. You cannot get there any faster; and at that age I doubt if your wealth--by which I mean the richness of your collected experience--will depend much on how many impressions you have been able to gather in quick succession. I am not saying that those impressions are worthless. But it seems likely that when they follow each other very rapidly each of them will cut a little less deep than the one before. And surely the most valuable part of one's mental baggage will always be made up of things which have taken time to happen: one's journey through the school years; the making of a garden; the growth of one's children. Those friendships which open and close in one season, however delightful, count for less, I think, than those which go on intermittently through the years. Love, in its largest meaning, is a thing of protracted growth, always revealing new depths, new kinds of understanding; and the satisfaction we get from lesser relationships--from our service to a firm or profession, for example--seems to be built up from a long series of adjustments, infinitely gradual changes.

You will agree, surely, that these slow and subtle processes are at least an ingredient in the happiness that is possible to human beings; and it is not hard to see that they can only be appreciated slowly. But, going a little further, I suggest that because we are creatures of very slow growth-- because until the day of our death we perhaps never reach maturity--it is important for us to be aware of those slow processes while they are occurring. Is it not possible that what they call 'the nervous strain of modern life' comes partly from the disconnection between the pace at which we receive impressions and the far slower pace at which we are able to absorb experience? Are our minds being geared to a speed which blurs reality? Are we missing the scenery-- losing something which is essential to our contentment and perhaps to our human dignity?

For myself, I cannot get away from the idea that the older kind of literature, the kind that explores life as a connoisseur would, taking its time, might still be of use in bridging that gap. To study other lives patiently, as that sort of literature does, might show us certain harmonies in our own which we have not had time to realise. But that is merely a hobby-horse of my own. It may well be that we have finally outgrown that sort of writing. And perhaps the deep satisfactions it represented, the poetry of quietness and slow accomplishment, are something we have outgrown as well.

INDEX

(The titles of Hutchinson's books are capitalized)